Casino Revenue Auditing

thomas rutledge

Published by thomas rutledge, 2024.

While every precaution has been taken in the preparation of this book, the publisher assumes no responsibility for errors or omissions, or for damages resulting from the use of the information contained herein.

CASINO REVENUE AUDITING

First edition. February 6, 2024.

Copyright © 2024 thomas rutledge.

ISBN: 979-8224358403

Written by thomas rutledge.

Table of Contents

Casino Revenue Auditing 1

Qualifications and Skills Needed 20

Audit Procedures and Techniques - A Guide 22

Cash Controls in Casinos - Why They Matter 28

Cash Counting and Verification Procedures 29

AML Measures in Casinos - Protecting Against Money Laundering 30

Slot Machine Auditing 32

Bingo and Other Unique Games 34

Hotel and Accommodation Revenue 36

Food and Beverage Sales 37

Entertainment and Event Revenue - The Facts 38

Casino Management Systems - An Overview 40

Auditing With Artificial Intelligence 42

Cybersecurity Measures in Revenue Auditing 43

Continuous Stakeholder Monitoring and Feedback 73

Continuous Training and Professional Development 74

Ethical Code for Revenue Auditors 76

Professional Skepticism and Due Professional Care 78

Enhanced Data Analytics 81

Enhanced Cybersecurity Measures 83

Integrating ESG Considerations into Your Business 85

Continued Professional Development 86

Casino Revenue Auditing

Thomas Rutledge CFE Retired, CICA, CBOM, BS, MBA

Published by Thomas Rutledge, 2024.

CASINO REVENUE AUDITING

First edition. February 6, 2024.

ISBN: 979-8224358403

Written by thomas rutledge.

Table of Contents

Casino Revenue Auditing

Qualifications and Skills Needed

Audit Procedures and Techniques - A Guide

Cash Controls in Casinos - Why They Matter

Cash Counting and Verification Procedures

AML Measures in Casinos - Protecting Against Money Laundering

Slot Machine Auditing

Bingo and Other Unique Games

Hotel and Accommodation Revenue

Food and Beverage Sales

Entertainment and Event Revenue - The Facts

Casino Management Systems - An Overview

Auditing With Artificial Intelligence

Cybersecurity Measures in Revenue Auditing

Continuous Stakeholder Monitoring and Feedback

Continuous Training and Professional Development

Ethical Code for Revenue Auditors

Professional Skepticism and Due Professional Care

Enhanced Data Analytics

Enhanced Cybersecurity Measures

Integrating ESG Considerations into Your Business

Continued Professional Development

CASINO REVENUE AUDITING

The Importance of Revenue Auditing in Casinos

Casinos are complex businesses with numerous revenue streams that require careful financial management. Revenue auditing plays a crucial role in safeguarding against fraudulent activities, mismanagement and errors which could negatively impact the casino's finances. By systematically reviewing transactions through an audit process transparency is maintained while ensuring security within this environment. The contribution made by these professionals cannot be overstated when it comes to maintaining sound fiscal practices for any gaming establishment.

Regulatory Compliance

The gaming industry is subject to an intricate web of regulations and compliance standards that are enforced by various authorities at different levels such as local, regional or national. For revenue auditors operating within this environment, it's crucial they have a comprehensive understanding of these rules. This section seeks to explain the complexities involved in navigating through these laws while highlighting how important revenue auditing plays in ensuring adherence with them all.

Casinos rely heavily on revenue auditors to safeguard their financial well-being. As gatekeepers of these establishments, they are responsible for ensuring compliance with stipulated regulations or face severe penalties and damage to the casino's reputation as a trustworthy business entity. The consequences of non-compliance cannot be overstated - it is crucial that all parties involved take this responsibility seriously.

The gaming industry is heavily regulated by various commissions that set standards for casino operations. These rules ensure fairness and transparency in all aspects of the business while also protecting against fraudulent activities within it. As revenue auditors are responsible for verifying financial transactions at these establishments, they must have a deep understanding of how each rule applies to their work so as not violate any laws or policies put forth by regulatory bodies. The importance placed on compliance with such guidelines cannot be overstated when considering one's role in this sector.

As revenue auditors, it is crucial that we remain cognizant of our reporting obligations. Our ability to provide accurate and timely financial records detailing revenues, expenses, and other transactions ensures transparency within the industry while maintaining accountability for ourselves as well as those around us. Failure in meeting these requirements could result in legal consequences or damage one's reputation among peers - something no one wants! Therefore, it is imperative that all professionals take this aspect seriously when working with finances related tasks at casinos.

The regulatory landscape is constantly evolving with new challenges and technological advancements emerging all the time. Revenue auditors must remain vigilant about these changes if they want to maintain compliance at all times. Proactive measures are essential in this context - embracing innovative methodologies and technology will help you stay ahead of any curveballs thrown your way. Stay adaptable and flexible so that you can navigate through changing regulations smoothly without hiccups or delays along the way!

The casino industry is subject to strict regulations that require compliance from all participants including revenue auditors. This mandate underscores the importance of proactive measures taken by these professionals in anticipating and adapting to future changes. By doing so they ensure not only financial integrity but also preserve their reputation as trustworthy entities within this competitive marketplace. Ultimately it comes down to being prepared for whatever may come next - an essential aspect when working with such high stakes!

Casino Business Models - An Overview

The gaming industry is characterized by a dynamic and complex landscape that necessitates an assortment of business models to cater for varying consumer preferences and market demands. From standalone casinos to sprawling resort complexes understanding these nuances is critical when auditing revenue within the sector. Individuals engaged in this process must be well versed with each model's intricacies if they are to achieve success.

Standalone casinos are an integral part of the gaming industry that have been around for years. These establishments may vary in size from small local venues to larger destination spots solely dedicated to providing quality gambling experiences. To audit revenue accurately within such settings requires a keen eye on financial transactions related specifically towards slot machines, table games and other wagering options available at these facilities. This process is critical since it forms the foundation upon which compliance verification takes place alongside accurate assessment results. Therefore, understanding each individual source of income generated by these activities remains paramount when conducting any form of auditing exercise within standalone casino environments.

Modern gaming has evolved beyond traditional casinos into expansive resort complexes that offer a wide range of amenities such as hotels, restaurants, entertainment venues and shopping centers. Auditing revenue in these types of establishments requires an extensive approach since earnings are generated not only from gambling activities but also through auxiliary services like hotel bookings or food sales. To ensure accurate financial reporting while adhering to regulatory compliance requirements auditors must delve deeply into all aspects of the business including non-gaming sources of income.

Auditing revenue in emerging forms of gambling such as online casinos and mobile gaming platforms requires an understanding of their unique business models. These platforms introduce additional layers of complexity including digital transactions, cybersecurity considerations and evolving regulatory frameworks specific to the online gaming sphere that need navigating by auditors. Its crucial for them to have a deep knowledge about these areas if they want accurate results from their work.

The role of revenue auditors in the gaming industry is not just about crunching numbers. It requires a deep understanding of how different business models operate within casinos - whether they are standalone establishments or expansive resort complexes. Auditors must be able to identify intricacies across various sources that contribute towards generating revenues such as traditional games and ancillary services. This knowledge enables them conduct thorough financial assessments while ensuring compliance with regulatory requirements; it also provides valuable insights into operational efficiency levels within this ever-evolving sector. Therefore, having skilled professionals who understand these nuances can make all the difference between success and failure for any establishment operating within this space. Casinos: The Standalone Experience

The gaming industry h as seen significant growth over the years with standalone casinos being a major contributor. These establishments offer an exclusive commitment to providing diverse and immersive experiences through their extensive array of attractions such as slot machines, table games or poker rooms. By focusing on specialized approaches towards gambling activities they cater precisely to patrons' preferences resulting in unique environments that are unmatched elsewhere within this competitive marketplace. Standalone casinos continue to be at forefront when it comes creating memorable moments for those seeking thrilling adventures!

Slot machines have long been a mainstay in standalone casinos offering players an opportunity to test their luck and potentially win big prizes. These gaming devices come in various forms from classic mechanical slots to sophisticated video slots with interactive features that contribute significantly towards the overall revenue of these establishments. The vibrant displays and distinctive sounds create an energetic atmosphere adding to the allure of standalone casinos as must visit destinations for anyone looking for thrilling entertainment options.

Standalone casinos offer a diverse range of gaming options that cater to different types of players. Table games like blackjack, roulette and craps are among the most popular choices for those seeking an interactive experience with other gamers while also enjoying the thrill of chance. Skilled dealers and croupiers add sophistication to these classic games by creating an environment where strategic gameplay is encouraged - making them even more appealing! Whether you're new or experienced at table games; standalone casinos have something special waiting just for you.

For those who love poker standalone casinos offer dedicated s paces that cater specifically to their needs. These rooms provide a range of different games including tournaments and cash games as well as opportunities for both novice players and seasoned professionals alike. The strategic nature o f t he game combined with social interactions at the table make these venues truly unique in terms of gaming experiences.

The versatility of standalone casinos is truly remarkable. In urban areas they serve as vibrant entertainment hubs that attract both locals and tourists seeking an exciting night out on the town. Meanwhile in rural regions these establishments offer a unique escape from daily routines providing individuals

4

with a retreat where they can fully immerse themselves into gaming entertainment without any distractions or interruptions caused by city life. The adaptability factor makes standalone casinos ideal for different settings while still maintaining their appeal among patrons looking to have fun!

Casinos have proven their worth by creating an environment that caters to the preferences of their target audience. These establishments are located in bustling urban centers or serene rural landscapes and aim at providing a tailored gaming experience for patrons who seek immersion into exhilarating entertainment options. As they continue evolving through innovation, standalone casinos remain essential contributors towards enriching diversity within the gaming industry with unique offerings that cannot be found elsewhere. With such dedication towards excellence, these institutions guarantee unforgettable experiences for all those seeking thrilling adventures on their premises!

Resort-Style Communities

Resort style casinos have revolutionized the gaming industry by offering an all-encompassing experience that goes beyond traditional boundaries. These expansive complexes redefine entertainment with their diverse range of amenities including hotels, restaurants shopping outlets and spas among others. They transform into destination resorts catering to a wide audience ranging from avid gamers to those who may not be interested in gambling at all! The inclusion of these additional features makes for a truly unique experience unlike anything else available today. With so much on offer it's no wonder why people keep coming back time after time!

The inclusion of hotels within resort style casinos offers a seamless transition from entertainment to relaxation. These luxurious accommodations provide guests with an immersive stay that is both comfortable and convenient. As revenue auditors in these complexes, it falls upon us to scrutinize not only the income generated by room bookings but also ancillary services such as spa treatments or other guest amenities.

The resort style casinos offer a wide range of dining options that cater to various preferences and tastes. Auditing revenue extends beyond gaming realms into examining financial transactions at restaurants including both casual eateries as well as fine-dining establishments. Revenue auditors must be meticulous in their analysis ensuring accuracy while adhering strictly to established accounting practices.

Shopping outlets within these complexes add another layer of complexity to revenue auditing. Retail stores and boutique shops generate income through the sale of merchandise. Auditors must keep track of all transactions related to retail sales ensuring that financial records accurately reflect this non-gaming activities earnings. This is crucial for maintaining transparency in finances across different sectors within a business or organization.

Resort style casinos with entertainment venues like theaters and concert halls present unique challenges for revenue auditors. Ticket sales, concession revenues as well as associated expenses all need to be carefully examined by these professionals who must possess both precision and flexibility when dealing with different types of income streams. The dynamic nature of such offerings demands constant vigilance from those tasked with ensuring financial accuracy in this industry sector.

The incorporation of spas and wellness facilities into resort style casinos necessitates additional financial considerations. Revenue auditors must carefully examine transactions related to these services such as fitness classes or wellness packages in order ensure that their records align with operational reality.

The intricate nature of resort style casinos necessitates a comprehensive approach towards revenue auditing. To ensure effective financial monitoring, management teams must implement robust systems that can handle diverse streams emanating from various aspects of the establishment. This oversight is not only crucial for regulatory compliance but also critical in optimizing profitability and operational efficiency within these large-scale entertainment complexes. In essence, revenue auditors play an integral role beyond just gaming operations by encompassing all services contributing to overall success and fiscal health at destination resorts.

Online Gaming Platforms

The gaming industry has undergone a significant transformation with the advent of technology and online casinos have emerged as one such pivotal component. These virtual platforms offer players unparalleled convenience by allowing them to access games from anywhere with internet connectivity. However, this presents auditors with unique challenges that require careful consideration - particularly6 when it comes to digital transactions, player data

security measures and keeping up-to-date on regulatory changes in real time. To navigate these intricacies successfully requires more than just understanding; its critical for auditors who want success in today's rapidly evolving landscape.

Auditors face a complex set of challenges when it comes to online gaming. The use of digital transactions encompassing various payment methods and virtual currencies necessitates advanced forensic techniques that can trace, verify and authenticate financial activities effectively. Additionally, the dynamic nature of these platforms requires constant vigilance against potential fraud or irregularities in finances. Auditing firms must be proactive about ensuring integrity within all aspects of their work while operating under strict regulations imposed by governing bodies worldwide.

Online gaming presents unique challenges when it comes to player data security. Auditors must carefully examine the measures taken by casinos to protect sensitive information from cyber threats and ensure compliance with regulatory requirements on privacy protection. The potential f or breaches necessitates stringent protocols that require auditors' expertise in digital security within this context.

The online gaming industry is constantly evolving due to changing regulations that require auditors' attention. Keeping up with modifications in licensing conditions, jurisdictional requirements and compliance standards ensures legal operations for casinos operating on the web. The global reach of these platforms adds another layer of complexity as auditors must navigate through diverse regulatory frameworks across different regions worldwide.

To effectively audit casino revenue streams across diverse business models financial professionals and auditors must possess a comprehensive understanding of each model's intricacies. Standalone casinos, resort style complexes, and online platforms present unique operational challenges that necessitate tailored approaches to assessment. While standalone casinos focus on traditional gaming activities resort style complexes encompass broad spectrum services while operating in physical spaces. Online platforms operate within digital landscapes with their own set of challenges such as cybersecurity threats or user privacy concerns. To conduct effective audits financial experts, need specialized knowledge about these nuances between different types of casinos. With this expertise they can ensure accurate reporting of revenues for stakeholders like investors or regulators who rely on trustworthy information when making decisions. Therefore, it is crucial for those working in finance related roles at casinos to stay up-to-date with the latest trends and developments affecting their industry so they may continue providing reliable results for all parties involved.

The intricacies of revenue auditing processes within the gaming industry require a deep understanding of different types of casino operations. This knowledge serves as an essential foundation for auditors who must navigate these complexities with precision and accuracy. Whether its assessing physical or digital environments - standalone casinos versus online platforms- nuanced approaches to auditing ensure transparency and trustworthiness in financial reporting while fostering integrity throughout this dynamic sector. By focusing on comprehensive analysis methods that take into account all aspects of each type of operation, auditors can provide accurate results that benefit both players and businesses alike. The result is greater confidence among stakeholders regarding fairness and honesty across every aspect of their interactions with the gaming world.

Casino Revenue Streams

Casinos are complex environments that generate revenue from a multitude of sources beyond what most people associate with gambling. In this section we delve into the intricate web of income streams that support casino operations and demonstrate how they extend far beyond traditional forms of wagering activities.

Gaming Operations

Slot machines are a staple in casinos and contribute significantly to their revenue. These automated gaming devices with flashing lights and engaging sounds lure players seeking both entertainment and the opportunity for substantial wins. With so much on offer it's no surprise why slot machines remain such an enduring attraction at casinos worldwide!

Table games such as blackjack, poker, roulette and craps are crucial sources of revenue for casinos. These classic favorites offer a social element that adds to the overall gaming experience making it appealing across different demographics. The vibrant atmosphere created by these games is what sets them apart from other forms of entertainment. With their unique blend of excitement and camaraderie they continue to be popular choices among players worldwide.

Accommodations and Hospitality

Casinos that operate integrated hotels and resorts offer luxurious accommodations to visitors. In addition to room bookings, revenue is generated from associated services such as spa treatments or other amenities. The combination of these factors makes for a truly immersive experience.

Food Experiences:

Casinos offer a diverse range of dining options from casual eateries to high end restaurants. Revenue auditors must carefully examine transactions related to these experiences and ensure that financial records are accurate. The scrutiny involved in this process requires attention to detail and expertise in accounting principles. It is crucial for revenue auditors to maintain accuracy throughout their work so as not compromise the integrity of financial statements.

Entertainment Spots:

Casinos are known for their entertainment offerings such as concerts and shows. These events require careful financial assessments that take into account factors like ticket sales, concessions, and associated services revenue streams. The complexity of these calculations is a testament to the intricate nature of casino finances.

Shopping and Retail

Casinos often feature shopping outlets and retail spaces that contribute to their revenue through the sale of merchandise. Auditors must keep a close eye on transactions related to these sales in order to ensure financial accuracy.

Spa and Wellness Services

Wellness amenities such as spa services and fitness centers are a significant source of revenue for many businesses. Auditors play an essential role in ensuring that financial records associated with these offerings remain transparent and accurate. They delve into all relevant documents to ensure compliance with established standards. By doing so they help protect both customers' interests and the integrity of the company itself.

Corporate and Event Spaces: 7 Tips for Success

Casinos have discovered a new source of revenue by offering conference and event spaces. Auditors must evaluate transactions related to booking these facilities for corporate events, conferences or weddings. This presents an opportunity for casino owners to generate additional income while providing top notch services that meet their clients' needs. The auditing process ensures transparency in all financial dealings associated with this service.

Online Gaming Platforms - 8 Reasons Why You Should Try Them

In today's digital age online gaming platforms have become a staple. Auditors must navigate unique challenges related to managing player data security and adhering to ever changing regulations governing virtual transactions while also ensuring that all activities are conducted legally within the bounds of lawful conduct in this sector. This requires constant vigilance from auditing professionals who work tirelessly behind the scenes keeping everything running smoothly for players around the world.

Loyalty Programs and Promotions:

Casinos frequently offer loyalty programs and promotions to encourage customer engagement. Auditors must monitor the financial impact of these initiatives on overall revenue.

Additional Services:

Casinos that offer transportation services such as shuttle buses or partnerships with local providers are subject to auditor scrutiny when it comes to transactions related to these ancillary services. These measures ensure transparency and accountability in the casino industry.

CASINO REVENUE AUDITING

The casino industries financial professionals must have a deep understanding of its diverse revenue streams if they want to succeed. These elements come together in an intricate tapestry that shapes the success and sustainability of these businesses ensuring their ability to adapt as needed in this ever-changing landscape. With such complexity at play it is crucial for those working within this sector to master auditing techniques so they can make informed decisions about how best allocate resources moving forward.

Sports Betting

The legalization of sports betting has created new challenges for revenue auditors. Understanding the financial implications associated with running a bookmaker operation - including odds, wagers and payouts - is essential in this evolving landscape. More over integrating technology into these platforms requires that auditing procedures adapt to digital dimensions while maintaining accuracy in reported revenues. As such it is important for professionals working within this industry sector to stay up-to-date on best practices when it comes to managing finances effectively amidst changing regulations and technological advancements alike.

Revenue auditors face a challenging task when navigating the diverse world of casino gaming. Each game type presents its own set of financial implications that require expertise and experience to navigate effectively. By developing effective audit procedures tailored specifically for each game type, revenue auditors can ensure accurate reporting while maintaining integrity within this dynamic industry. The ability to adapt quickly is key in such an ever-changing environment as the one found inside any casino establishment!

As a revenue auditor in the casino industry, one must possess an intricate understanding of finance along with exceptional attention to detail. This section explores what defines this role and its core responsibilities.

The text should be written concisely yet effectively using language that is easy for anyone to understand: The job description of being a revenue auditor at any gaming establishment requires extensive knowledge about financial matters as well as keen observation skills. With these qualities combined with expertise on how things work within the unique environment of casinos; such professionals are able to make accurate assessments while ensuring fairness among all parties involved. Their primary tasks include monitoring cash flow systems closely while identifying potential areas where improvements can be made or fraudulent activities may occur. Additionally, they also play a crucial part in verifying tax returns submitted by players accurately reflecting their winnings/losses during gameplay sessions. Ultimately, it's up to them whether certain transactions meet legal requirements before finalizing payments between both sides. By fulfilling these duties diligently every day - revenue auditors help maintain transparency & trustworthiness across all aspects of casino operations.

Verification of Financial Transactions

The revenue auditor plays a critical role in maintaining the financial integrity of casinos. They are responsible for examining various sources that generate income such as traditional cash transactions and modern electronic payment methods with precision. The ultimate goal is to ensure accuracy, transparency while eliminating any errors or inconsistencies that could compromise the reputation and stability of the establishment. This position requires diligence and attention to detail as it holds significant implications on how well-run operations function within this industry. Therefore, having skilled professionals who can handle these responsibilities effectively is crucial for success.

Analysis of Revenue Streams:

Cash transactions constitute a substantial portion of casino revenue. To ensure accuracy in recording these transactions, revenue auditors carefully examine every transaction at gaming tables and slot machines as well as other points of service. This meticulous scrutiny ensures that all cash exchanges are accurately reflected within the financial system.

Credit card payments are a popular method of payment in casinos and auditors take great care to ensure their accuracy. This involves verifying charges, confirming proper authorization, and reconciling transactions with financial records. The process is critical for maintaining transparency and preventing fraudulent activity within the gaming industry.

Technology has revolutionized the way we make payments with electronic methods like digital wallets and online transfers becoming increasingly popular.

Revenue auditors are tasked with navigating these complex transactions to ensure they're securely processed while also accurately recorded.

Maintaining Accuracy and Consistency:

Auditors don't just look at the numbers; they verify each transaction by cross referencing it with supporting documentation. This includes receipts, vouchers and other records of transactions to ensure their legitimacy.

Auditing involves a detailed examination of financial records that enables identification of any discrepancies, irregularities or anomalies. This proactive approach helps prevent escalation by addressing potential issues early on. By taking this meticulous approach auditors ensure accuracy and reliability in their findings.

Auditors are responsible for conducting meticulous reconciliation processes that match recorded revenues with actual cash counts and other forms of payment. Any inconsistencies or disparities discovered during this process require thorough investigation to ensure financial accuracy remains intact.

Maintaining High Financial Standards:

Casinos operate in a highly regulated environment where compliance with gaming laws and financial reporting standards is paramount. Revenue auditors play an essential role ensuring adherence to these rules imposed by relevant authorities. Their efforts are critical for maintaining transparency and accountability within the industry.

Auditors play a critical role in mitigating risks by conducting thorough audits. By identifying and rectifying discrepancies early on they help prevent financial discrepancies that could lead to legal or reputational damage. Their efforts contribute significantly towards building robust risk management strategies for organizations.

The handling of financial matters by revenue auditors highlights the significance of upholding high standards for integrity and trustworthiness within gaming establishments. This helps build a positive reputation as an honest and transparent casino that people can rely on. The meticulousness displayed in this process is essential to maintaining such values.

The role of a revenue auditor in casinos is not limited to crunching numbers. It extends beyond that into ensuring the accuracy, consistency and compliance of all financial transactions within these establishments. This meticulous process serves as an essential safeguard against any potential issues with regards to finances while also upholding trust among patrons and regulatory authorities alike regarding the integrity of gaming industries across various regions worldwide. Maintaining high standards when it comes down handling money matters isn't just about fulfilling obligations; its about making a commitment towards operating ethically and transparently - something which should be at the forefront for every single player involved within this industry sector today!

Compliance Monitoring:

Casinos rely heavily on revenue auditors to ensure they are adhering both internally and externally. These professionals must possess a comprehensive understanding of gaming regulations, AML laws as well as other relevant statutes in order for them to effectively carry out their duties. Through regular audits any potential compliance issues can be identified quickly so that necessary measures may be taken before things get out of hand or become problematic later down the line. This way casino operations remain within legal boundaries at all times without compromising quality service delivery.

Assessing Internal Controls

The revenue auditor plays a critical role in assessing and fortifying internal controls. This entails evaluating the effectiveness of measures put in place to protect assets, prevent fraudulent activities from occurring while ensuring accurate financial reporting is maintained at all times. Auditors may recommend improvements based on their observations as well as industry best practices for better control mechanisms within an organization's system.

Documentation and Reporting:

Effective revenue auditing requires meticulous documentation practices. Auditors maintain detailed records of their examinations, findings and recommendations throughout the process. This ensures that clear concise reports can be generated for relevant stakeholders such as management teams or regulatory authorities to review. These reports serve an essential purpose in driving continuous improvement through corrective action plans based on these results.

Qualifications and Skills Needed

Financial Acumen:

A revenue auditor must possess a strong foundation in financial principles to succeed. This requires proficiency with accounting principles, financial analysis techniques and the ability to interpret complex data sets accurately. Working knowledge of casino industry specific documents such as ledgers or statements is also essential for success in this role. With these skills under their belt an effective auditor can ensure that all transactions are conducted fairly and legally while maintaining compliance standards set by regulatory bodies.

Analytical Skills

The ability to analyze data and detect anomalies is a vital skill for revenue auditors. They must be able to identify irregularities in financial transactions assess the effectiveness of internal controls make informed recommendations for improvement while dealing with diverse revenue streams present at casinos. Analytical skills are particularly crucial when working within this industry where accuracy matters most.

Attention to Detail

The intricate nature of financial transactions in casinos necessitates a keen eye for detail. Revenue auditors must diligently review vast amounts of data to ensure accuracy and completeness at all times. Any oversight could have severe consequences on both regulatory compliance and financial reporting alike. Accordingly, it is crucial that revenue auditors remain vigilant throughout their workday.

Communication Skills

Effective communication is a critical competency for revenue auditors. They must be able to articulate complex financial concepts in an understandable and concise manner, both through written reports as well as verbal presentations. Strong communication skills enable collaboration with various stakeholders such as casino management teams, regulatory agencies or external and internal audit groups.

Ethical Issues in Casino Auditing

Maintaining high ethical standards is a fundamental aspect of being an effective revenue auditor. This section delves into the various considerations that come with casino auditing, emphasizing on integrity, objectivity and confidentiality as key pillars for success in this role. Auditors must navigate potential conflicts while adhering to professional codes of conduct; ultimately prioritizing what is best for both stakeholders involved - namely the casinos themselves!

The role of a revenue auditor is not just about crunching numbers; it involves much more than that. To excel in this position requires both technical proficiency and unwavering ethical standards to uphold the financial wellbeing as well as regulatory compliance for casinos. A successful revenue auditor must possess these qualities if they want to succeed in their job responsibilities effectively.

Audit Procedures and Techniques - A Guide

Pre-audit Preparation

A successful revenue audit requires careful preparation beforehand. This involves understanding the casinos' organizational structure and policies while identifying key risk areas that may need closer examination during the actual auditing process itself. The pre-audit phase also includes creating a detailed plan outlining objectives, scope, methodologies used in conducting this important task effectively. By taking these steps upfront revenue auditors can ensure an efficient systematic approach towards achieving their goals accurately within given timelines without any hiccups along the way!

Organizational Structure Explained

To conduct a successful pre audit preparation process, it is essential for auditors to have an in depth understanding of the casinos organizational structure. This includes familiarizing themselves with key departments within management hierarchies and reporting structures. By doing so they can identify potential areas that require attention during their audits while focusing on where risks may arise. The knowledge gained from this exercise ensures maximum efficiency when assessing any given situation beforehand.

Reviewing Policies and Procedures

Revenue auditors conduct a thorough examination of casinos internal policies and procedures with particular emphasis on those related to financial transactions, internal controls as well as compliance. This step ensures that they are fully aware of established protocols allowing them to assess adherence effectively while identifying any deviations during the audit process. The rewritten text should be between 47-141 words in length: Revenue auditing involves meticulously scrutinizing casino operations by focusing specifically on their internal control mechanisms for finance management or regulatory requirements. By doing so auditors gain an understanding of how things work within these organizations which helps them identify potential issues more accurately when carrying out audits later on down the line. Through this approach they can ensure maximum efficiency at all times without compromising quality standards whatsoever!

Identifying and Assessing Risk

Preparing for an audit requires careful consideration of potential risks within casino operations. Auditors evaluate the complexity and volume of gaming activities as well as assess existing internal controls to develop effective procedures that address these challenges head on. This risk centric approach ensures comprehensive coverage during every stage of the process. By prioritizing risk identification beforehand, audits can be more efficient while minimizing any surprises or unexpected findings later down the line.

Audit Planning - The Basics

A well thought out audit plan is essential for a successful revenue auditing process. The planning phase involves defining the scope of investigation along with specific areas that require attention from experts in this field. Additionally, it includes developing an appropriate methodology by selecting suitable sampling techniques and testing frequencies while also establishing criteria to evaluate internal controls effectiveness accurately. This approach ensures thoroughness during investigations while minimizing errors or oversights that could impact results negatively. Therefore, having a comprehensive audit plan guarantees better accuracy when assessing financial statements' validity and reliability ultimately leading towards improved decision-making processes within organizations based on accurate information provided through these evaluations.

Revenue Verification Sampling Methods

The sheer scale of transactions within a casino makes it impossible for auditors to verify every single one. Instead, they rely on sampling techniques that allow them to confirm the accuracy of financial records without examining each and every transaction in detail. This section explores various methods used by revenue auditing experts when conducting their investigations.

Random Sampling: A Definition

Random sampling involves selecting a subset of transactions at random from the entire population. This method ensures that each transaction has an equal chance of being included in the sample and provides a representative viewpoint on irregularities across different transactions. By using this approach, it becomes easier to identify deviations or anomalies within the data set without any bias towards specific groups or individuals. The effectiveness of random sampling lies in its ability to provide unbiased results while still capturing important information about the overall population under study.

Stratified Sampling - What It Is

Auditors can use stratified sampling to divide a population into smaller groups based on specific criteria such as transaction type or time period. This approach allows for more targeted examination and ensures that each subgroup is given adequate representation in the sample size. By doing so auditors are able better understand potential risks within these subgroups while also providing greater accuracy when analyzing overall results from their testing efforts. Over-all this methodology provides valuable insights into areas where further investigation may be necessary leading towards improved decision-making processes downstream.

Systematic Sampling: A Brief Overview

Systematic sampling involves selecting every nth item from a sorted list of transactions. This method is both efficient and straightforward, providing an organized approach to sample selection. It proves particularly useful when dealing with chronologically ordered transactions.

Judgmental Sampling

Judgmental sampling is a technique used by auditors where they rely on their professional judgment to select specific transactions for examination based on perceived risks or anomalies. This method enables them to focus primarily on high-risk areas and transactions that may indicate potential issues with greater accuracy than other methods available at the time. The subjective nature of this approach allows for flexibility in decision making while still maintaining an effective level of precision when it comes down to detecting irregularities within financial records.

Examining Financial Statements and Records

Revenue auditing involves a thorough examination of financial statements and records. Auditors scrutinize these documents to ensure their accuracy, completeness, and adherence to accounting principles. This section provides an overview of the key aspects involved in this process.

Financial Statement Review

Financial statements are subjected to intense scrutiny by auditors who examine every aspect of them including the income statement, balance sheet and cash flow statement. This involves assessing whether revenue figures accurately reflect reality along with expense allocations while also evaluating how well-presented financial information is overall. Any inconsistencies or discrepancies found during this process will be further investigated for clarification purposes.

Transaction Verification

Revenue auditors conduct a thorough examination of individual transactions by scrutinizing supporting documentation such as invoices, receipts and electronic records. This meticulous process ensures that each transaction is validated for its authenticity authorized correctly before being recorded accurately within the financial statements.

Reconciliation Procedures:

Financial statement examination requires auditors to conduct thorough reconciliation procedures on various accounts such as cash, receivables and payables. This process ensures that the balances reported in these statements match up with their supporting records accurately. By doing so any discrepancies can be identified quickly allowing for prompt resolutions before they become larger issues down the line.

Accounting Standards Compliance

The auditors' examination involves assessing the casinos adherence to relevant accounting standards and principles. This entails verifying that revenue recognition follows established guidelines, expenses are accurately classified according to their nature, and accounting policies remain consistent throughout all transactions.

The Importance of Electronic Data Analysis in Casino Auditing

The use of technology has transformed the way casinos operate and revenue auditors have adapted accordingly by utilizing electronic data analysis techniques to optimize their auditing processes. This approach allows for greater efficiency and effectiveness in identifying potential issues or discrepancies within financial records. As such it is becoming increasingly important that those responsible for overseeing these operations are well versed in this methodology so they can stay ahead of any potential challenges.

Data Mining: What It Is and How to Use It

Revenue auditors leverage data mining to uncover patterns and insights from large datasets. By doing so they can identify trends, anomalies, as well as potential areas of risk within casinos financial information. This technique is particularly effective in detecting irregularities in transaction patterns.

Data Analytics Tools: A Guide

Auditors use specialized data analytics tools to quickly process and analyze vast amounts of financial information. These instruments enable them to detect outliers, unusual trends or potential discrepancies that require further investigation. With the help of these advanced technologies auditors can uncover hidden patterns and irregularities more effectively than ever before.

Transaction Monitoring Systems - A Guide

Casinos have implemented transaction monitoring systems to detect and flag suspicious activities. Revenue auditors work alongside these systems by examining alerts, investigating questionable transactions while ensuring compliance with AML regulations. These measures contribute significantly towards maintaining the integrity of financial operations within casino establishments.

The chapter emphasizes the significance of meticulous pre audit preparations, effective sampling methods usage during examination of financial statements and incorporation of electronic data analysis techniques in revenue auditing. These procedures constitute a robust framework for auditors to navigate through complexities present within casino environments while ensuring accuracy and integrity of financial reporting.

Managing Cash - Tips and Techniques

In casinos where millions of dollars change hands daily cash management is crucial for ensuring financial stability. This chapter delves into the intricate processes involved in managing cash within a gaming establishment and underscores how critical it is to implement strict controls that protect assets while maintaining transparency.

Cash Controls in Casinos - Why They Matter

Financial Safeguarding

Cash is indispensable for any casino's survival and prosperity. To ensure that this vital resource remains secure from theft, fraud or errors in cash-related transactions robust controls are essential. The ability of a casino to maintain security and accuracy with regards to these types of transactions has significant implications on its overall financial health. Therefore, it goes without saying that effective management of cash flow should be given utmost priority by all stakeholders involved in running such establishments.

Cash Handling Internal Controls

The success of casinos hinges on their ability to manage cash effectively. To achieve this goal revenue auditors, collaborate with management teams in establishing and enforcing internal controls such as segregation of duties, dual authorization for large transactions or regular reconciliations among others. These measures act as safeguards against both intentional misconducts and unintentional errors that could compromise the integrity of operations within these institutions. By implementing robust control mechanisms casino operators can ensure optimal performance while minimizing risks associated with financial losses due to fraudulent activities or mistakes made by staff members. Therefore, investing time into creating effective policies around managing money is crucial if one wants to succeed in running a profitable gaming establishment over an extended period of time.

Cash Counting and Verification Procedures

The Importance of Regular Cash Counts

Cash counting is a fundamental aspect of casino operations that requires regular and unpredictable checks. Revenue auditors oversee these procedures to ensure they are conducted by qualified personnel using established protocols. The frequency and randomness of cash counts contribute significantly towards enhancing control measures effectiveness.

Cash Handling Procedures Verification

Auditors play a crucial role in ensuring that cash handling procedures are functioning properly by verifying their accuracy. This involves examining documentation associated with each transaction and comparing it against the actual amount of money on hand. Any inconsistencies or discrepancies will be thoroughly investigated until root causes have been identified. The auditor's work is essential for maintaining transparency within financial institutions

.

AML Measures in Casinos - Protecting Against Money Laundering

AML Compliance

Casinos are subject to strict anti-money laundering regulations as financial institutions. This section examines the measures in place within casinos for detecting and preventing illicit financial activities such as customer due diligence, transaction monitoring and reporting suspicious activity to regulatory authorities. Auditors play a critical role assessing these measures' effectiveness. It is imperative that they do so accurately give their impact on maintaining transparency and integrity within this industry

Employee Training and Awareness

Casinos must prioritize staff training on AML procedures to ensure compliance with regulations. Revenue auditors evaluate the effectiveness of these programs by emphasizing employee awareness and reporting capabilities for suspicious transactions. By fostering a culture that values adherence to rules through comprehensive training initiatives casino management can promote accountability among their workforce while upholding regulatory requirements.

Cash Management and Technology Innovations
Cash Management Systems - What You Need to Know

Modern casinos have embraced advanced cash management systems that integrate technology to streamline processes. Revenue auditors evaluate these technologies by assessing their potential for enhancing efficiency, accuracy and security in handling money. The seamless integration with other casino management systems ensures a smooth flow of financial data.

Automating Cash Handling

The use of automation has become increasingly prevalent in cash handling processes. This section delves into how casinos utilize technologies such as smart safes, RFID tracking systems and cash counting machines to streamline various aspects of managing their finances electronically. The reliability and security measures implemented by these tools are assessed by revenue auditors who aim at mitigating risks associated with manual cash management methods.

Blockchain and Cryptocurrencies: A Beginner's Guide

Casinos are exploring the potential of blockchain technology and cryptocurrencies as a means to enhance their cash management processes. Revenue auditors evaluate these options by examining how they could impact transactions while also considering any associated risks or controls that may arise from using digital currencies instead of traditional methods. The decentralized nature of blockchain offers an opportunity for greater transparency in financial operations within casinos. With this emerging trend, there is hope that new possibilities will be discovered through innovative technologies like blockchain.

In conclusion this chapter highlights the critical role that effective cash management plays in maintaining financial stability and integrity within casinos. By examining their procedures for handling money closely enforcing robust internal controls adapting to technological advancements revenue auditors contribute significantly towards enhancing overall security while also improving efficiency levels within a dynamic environment like those found at casinos.

Gaming Revenue Audit

The world of casinos is complex and intricate with gaming activities being at its core. To ensure that these transactions are accurate and honest revenue auditors employ specialized techniques and procedures known as gaming revenue audit. This chapter delves into the nuances involved in this process highlighting how it helps maintain transparency within an industry where trust is paramount.

Slot Machine Auditing

RNG Verification - Is It Random?

Casinos are renowned for their slot machines, which rely on RNGs to ensure fair and random outcomes. Revenue auditors play a crucial role in verifying the proper functioning of these systems so that players can rest assured knowing they're getting an authentic experience with every spin.

Payout Percentage Analysis

Slot machine payout percentages are subject to scrutiny by auditors who ensure that they adhere to regulatory requirements and casino policies. This involves comparing actual payments with theoretical ones based on the machines design parameters.

Jackpot Verification Process

Large jackpots are a major attraction for many casino goers. Auditors carefully verify payouts ensuring that they adhere to predetermined rules and maintain accurate records for taxation purposes. This meticulous process guarantees fairness in the disbursement of winnings while also satisfying regulatory requirements.

Chip Counting and Verification: A Guide

The use of gaming chips is an integral part of table games and revenue auditors play a crucial role in ensuring their accuracy by conducting regular counts and verifications. This process involves reconciling chip inventories with recorded transactions while identifying any inconsistencies that may arise during the count. It's essential for casinos to maintain accurate records as it helps prevent fraudulent activities from occurring within their establishment.

Pit Procedures Examination:

The revenue auditors' primary focus is on the casino pits where table games are hosted. They carefully observe dealer actions to ensure compliance with gaming regulations and verify that all transactions recorded during gameplay are accurate. The procedures employed in these areas undergo intense scrutiny by experts who aim for transparency and fairness in every aspect of gambling operations.

Card Shuffling and Dealing Protocols

For card-based table games like blackjack and poker auditors scrutinize the shuffling protocols to ensure fairness. They assess whether or not dealers are adhering to established rules by monitoring their actions while also checking if any irregularities exist within card shuffling machines. This ensures that players have an equal chance at winning without interference from external factors.

Rake Collection Verification Process

In poker rooms revenue auditors play a crucial role in ensuring that rake collection procedures are accurate and fair. They verify the correctness of these processes by checking if established rates have been followed properly while also confirming whether proper documentation has been maintained throughout this process. This helps maintain transparency within gaming operations while safeguarding players' interests as well. Tournament Fees - A Breakdown

When it comes to poker tournaments auditors take a close look at the fees associated with buy ins and rebuys. They verify that these calculations are accurate and ensure compliance with both casino policies as well as regulatory standards. This is an important aspect of ensuring fairness in gaming operations.

Player Account Reconciliation

In poker rooms where player accounts are prevalent auditors play a crucial role in reconciling these accounts. They cross reference financial records with player transactions to ensure that funds are accurately credited and debited. This process is essential for maintaining transparency within the gaming industry.

Bingo and Other Unique Games

Verify Phone Numbers:

For games like bingo where random number calling is paramount auditors are responsible for verifying the integrity of these procedures. This entails confirming that proper functioning random number generators are being used and ensuring adherence to gaming regulations.

Analyzing Payout Structures

Specialty games require meticulous attention to detail when it comes to their payout structures. Revenue auditors play a crucial role in ensuring that these align with regulatory standards and predetermined rules set by casinos themselves. This involves examining game rules, verifying calculations for accuracy as well as confirming proper recording of all winnings won or lost during playtime. The work done by revenue auditors is critical towards maintaining fairness across different types of gaming experiences offered at various locations within the industry.

Confirming Randomness in Game Outcomes

In specialty games that involve chance auditors play a crucial role in ensuring fairness by confirming the randomness of game outcomes. This involves verifying algorithms governing electronic games or checking physical components like wheels and dice for any biases. The integrity of these games relies heavily on this process being done accurately and thoroughly.

The intricacies of gaming revenue require specialized audit procedures and techniques. This chapter delves into these nuances as it pertains to slot machines, table games, poker rooms, and other unique offerings within casinos. The role played by revenue auditors in maintaining the integrity of operations cannot be overstated - they are essential for ensuring fairness and transparency across all areas of play.

Non-Gaming Revenue Audit

CASINO REVENUE AUDITING

While gaming activities are a major source of revenue for casinos non-gaming elements such as hotel accommodations, food and beverage services, and entertainment also play an important role. In this chapter we examine the unique audit procedures involved in overseeing these additional streams of income.

Hotel and Accommodation Revenue

Room Rate Verification

Revenue auditors are meticulous in verifying the accuracy of room rates charged to guests. This involves cross referencing reservation records, checking rate adjustments and ensuring that any promotional offers or discounts have been applied correctly. Both financial transparency and customer satisfaction rely on accurate room rate verification.

Occupancy Rate Analysis

Hotel auditors play a crucial role in maximizing revenue by monitoring occupancy rates during peak periods and adjusting pricing strategies accordingly. By doing so they can optimize profits while identifying areas for improvement. Keeping tabs on these metrics is essential for any successful hotel operation.

Ancillary Service Revenue Verification

Beyond simply offering accommodations hotels generate additional revenue through services like room service spa treatments and parking. Revenue auditors play a crucial role in verifying the accuracy of these charges ensuring that they match up with what was provided while also being properly recorded on financial statements.

Food and Beverage Sales

Sales Verification:

The role of revenue auditors in casinos is crucial as they scrutinize sales records from food and beverage outlets within the establishment. This involves verifying transaction accuracy, confirming menu prices, reconciling sales figures with inventory records while also ensuring that discounts or promotions are correctly applied without any errors whatsoever. The importance of this process cannot be overstated since it helps maintain transparency and accountability for all parties involved.

Inventory Controls - What You Need to Know

Effective inventory control is paramount in food and beverage operations. Auditors assess the accuracy of inventory counts, verify recorded levels against physical stocks, and identify any inconsistencies that may indicate issues such as spoilage or pilfering. By doing so they help ensure smooth operation and profitability for businesses within this industry sector.

Health and Safety Compliance

Food and beverage revenue auditors work alongside health and safety inspectors to ensure compliance with regulatory standards. This entails verifying that food handling, storage, and preparation practices adhere to strict guidelines for hygiene and safety. Collaborating closely on this front is essential in maintaining high quality products while protecting consumers from potential risks associated with contaminated or unsafe foods.

Entertainment and Event Revenue - The Facts

Ticket Sales Verification

Casinos that offer live entertainment and events rely on revenue auditors to verify their ticket sales. This entails cross checking records of ticket sales with actual attendance figures confirming the accuracy of pricing while ensuring compliance with regulatory requirements.

Auditing Concession Revenue

Revenue auditors play a crucial role in ensuring that events run smoothly by examining concession sales. They verify the accuracy of records and implement measures to prevent any mismanagement or fraudulent activity. With their expertise, they ensure fairness for all parties involved while also protecting against financial losses due to negligence.

Profitability Analysis

Auditors may also evaluate the profitability of entertainment and events by conducting a comprehensive financial analysis. This involves taking into account all expenses such as artist fees, venue costs, and promotional spending to determine their overall impact on revenue generation.

Cross-Verification and Integration of Non-Gaming Revenue Streams

Recognizing the interconnectedness of non-gaming revenue streams is a key aspect for revenue auditors. To ensure consistency across different departments they perform cross verification by confirming that transactions related to hotel stays, dining and entertainment align seamlessly. This results in accurate financial reporting.

Auditing non-gaming revenue streams within a casino presents unique challenges and considerations. The role of revenue auditors is crucial in ensuring financial operations beyond the gaming floor are accurate, transparent, and compliant with regulations. Their work plays an essential part in maintaining trust among stakeholders while safeguarding against fraudulent activities.

CASINO REVENUE AUDITING

Casino Revenue Auditing - Technology and Software

The rapid advancement of technology has caused a significant shift in the casino industry leading to changes in how revenue auditing is conducted. This chapter delves into integrating specialized software tools and technology within these processes highlighting their critical role in enhancing efficiency, accuracy as well as compliance levels

Casino Management Systems - An Overview

Integrated Solutions:

Modern casinos have adopted sophisticated Casino Management Systems (CMS) that integrate various operational aspects such as gaming, hotel management and customer relationship management. Revenue auditors scrutinize the functionalities of CMS to comprehend how these systems capture process and report financial transactions across different departments. The integration between these functions allows for seamless operations within a single platform while ensuring accurate reporting at all times.

The Importance of Data Centralization

Casinos generate vast amounts of data from various sources that need to be analyzed by auditors. Centralizing this information through CMS simplifies the process for them as it provides a comprehensive view of financial activities across all departments within the casino. This section delves into how leveraging centralized data helps streamline audit procedures, improve accuracy levels and facilitate cross verification processes.

Automated Data Analysis

Audit software and tools provide auditors with the ability to automate data analysis, enabling them to quickly examine large datasets. These resources aid in identifying patterns, anomalies, as well as potential areas of risk by applying specific algorithms for transaction data evaluation. With these capabilities at their disposal auditors can work more efficiently than ever before.

Exception Reporting:

Audit software incorporates exception reporting features that draw attention to transactions or activities outside established norms. This enables auditors to focus their efforts on areas requiring further investigation resulting in a more targeted and efficient process overall. By leveraging these capabilities, businesses can streamline compliance processes while ensuring adherence with regulatory requirements.

Continuous Monitoring

The integration of continuous monitoring tools enables auditors to keep tabs on financial transactions in real time. This proactive approach empowers them with the ability to detect irregularities immediately and take corrective

action promptly before they escalate into major issues that could impact finances negatively. With this system in place, companies can rest assured knowing their financials are being monitored continuously for any potential discrepancies or errors

.

Auditing With Artificial Intelligence

Predictive Analytics: What It Is and How It Can Help Your Business

Auditors are increasingly turning to artificial intelligence (AI) and machine learning algorithms for predictive analytics in revenue auditing. These technologies enable them to forecast future trends identify potential risks proactively address emerging issues before they become major problems. With this approach auditors can stay ahead of the curve and ensure their clients financial well-being is protected at all times.

Detecting Fraud

AI has revolutionized fraud detection capabilities within revenue auditing by providing unparalleled precision and accuracy. Machine learning algorithms can analyze patterns in transaction data to identify unusual behaviors and flag potentially fraudulent activities with ease. This section delves into how auditors use AI tools to bolster their defenses against financial crimes.

Speech and Text Analysis

Natural language processing (NLP) has revolutionized the way auditors analyze spoken and written interactions. By utilizing this technology casino operations can gain valuable insights into potential areas of concern or improvement by analyzing customer feedback, employee communications and other textual data. With NLP at their disposal auditors are better equipped than ever before to ensure that all aspects of a casino's operation run smoothly.

Cybersecurity Measures in Revenue Auditing

Data Security Protocols

In todays' digital age cybersecurity is a critical consideration for auditors. This section delves into the various measures implemented in revenue auditing to protect sensitive financial data from unauthorized access and potential threats posed by hackers or other malicious actors online.

Secure Data Transmission: How to Keep Your Information Safe

In todays' digital age revenue auditing requires secure transmission of data between systems, especially when using cloud-based solutions or sharing information with external stakeholders. Robust encryption protocols and secure data transmission practices are critical components in ensuring cybersecurity during these processes.

Cybersecurity Training for Employees

Auditors may evaluate the effectiveness of employee training programs on cybersecurity awareness by assessing their ability to educate casino staff about best practices for data protection and recognizing phishing attempts. Additionally, they must ensure that employees adhere strictly to secure protocols in all aspects of their daily tasks. This is crucial given the potential risks associated with cyber threats.

In summary this chapter underscores the critical role of technology in reshaping casino revenue auditing. By leveraging advanced software tools, artificial intelligence and cybersecurity measures auditors can optimize their efficiency while navigating through an ever-changing gaming industry landscape. This integration ensures that they remain at the forefront of innovation within their field.

Casino Revenue Auditing and Regulatory Compliance

The casino industry operates within a highly regulated environment that requires adherence to various laws, standards and oversight bodies. This chapter delves into the critical role played by revenue auditors in ensuring strict compliance with regulatory requirements while safeguarding the integrity of the establishment as well as maintaining trust among patrons and authorities alike.

Casino Regulations

The regulatory environment for casinos is intricate and constantly evolving, comprising various laws, standards, as well as oversight mechanisms meant to ensure that gaming activities are conducted fairly, responsibly while maintaining integrity. Revenue auditors within these establishments play a critical role in navigating through this complex framework by adhering strictly to its guidelines.

This section delves into some of the key elements influencing casino revenue auditing due to their impact on regulation.

Gaming Regulations:

Casinos must abide by strict licensing requirements set forth by regulatory authorities in order to operate legally. Revenue auditors play a crucial role here as they scrutinize these permits and ensure that casinos adhere strictly to the conditions laid out by their respective licensors. Without proper documentation or compliance with regulations, businesses could face severe consequences such as fines or even closure.

Game fairness and integrity are critical components of any successful casino operation. Regulations outline specific standards for each type of game offered on site; auditors then conduct thorough assessments to ensure that these rules are being followed accurately by all parties involved in gaming activities at the establishment. This ensures an even playing field where players have a realistic chance of winning while also maintaining acceptable house edge percentages within permissible limits set forth by lawmakers. By prioritizing transparency through rigorous testing methods, casinos can foster trust among patrons who know they're getting a fair shot every time they play their favorite games!

Casinos are subject to regulatory compliance audits by external bodies. To facilitate this process revenue auditors within the casino work closely with these external auditors providing access to financial records and other relevant information. This collaboration ensures that all necessary measures have been taken towards meeting legal requirements.

Anti-Money Laundering Laws

AML laws necessitate that casinos implement robust customer due diligence procedures. Revenue auditors evaluate the effectiveness of these measures by examining whether or not they verify customers' identities monitor transactions and report suspicious activities. These evaluations ensure compliance with legal requirements while safeguarding against potential risks associated with money laundering.

Auditors assess casinos' transaction monitoring systems to ensure they can detect and report any unusual financial activity. This includes examining the implementation of technology tools that identify potential money laundering or other illicit activities. The auditor will also evaluate how well these measures are being executed by the casino staff. By doing so, they aim at keeping gambling establishments safe from criminal elements seeking to exploit their services for personal gain.

AML regulations impose strict record-keeping obligations on casinos. Auditors verify that these establishments maintain comprehensive records of financial transactions, customer identification and AML related communications to ensure compliance with the law.

Responsible Gaming Practices: Compliance

Regulatory frameworks often prioritize player protection by implementing responsible gaming practices. These measures include self-exclusion programs, age verification tools and managing gambling limits among others. Revenue auditors evaluate their effectiveness in safeguarding players from any negative impacts associated with gambling activities.

Casinos are held accountable for their advertising and marketing efforts through regulatory guidelines. Auditors evaluate promotional materials to ensure that they adhere to these standards, protecting individuals from exploitation by misleading campaigns. By enforcing responsible practices in this area casino operators can promote fairness while maintaining transparency with customers.

International and Local Standards

The regulatory landscape for casinos varies significantly across different countries and regions. Revenue auditors must be well versed in both international standards as well as local regulations to navigate through the complexities of operating within diverse jurisdictions. This requires a deep understanding of how these two factors interact with each other when it comes time for financial reporting or compliance checks. With this knowledge at hand revenue auditors can ensure that their clients are always following all necessary rules while still maximizing profits wherever possible.

Auditors are always up to date with the latest industry best practices which may serve as de facto standards when explicit regulations do not exist. By adopting these practices casinos ensure that they meet regulatory requirements while also adhering to high ethical conduct. This is essential for maintaining trust among customers and stakeholders alike.

The role of revenue auditors in the casino industry is complex due to intricate regulatory requirements. To ensure compliance with existing rules while staying ahead of updates requires constant vigilance from these professionals. Through their diligent efforts they contribute significantly towards maintaining trustworthiness and integrity within financial operations at casinos across various jurisdictions worldwide. The importance of this cannot be overstated as it helps protect both players' interests along with those who invest in gaming companies listed on stock exchanges globally. Therefore, it is crucial that all stakeholders work together towards achieving a common goal - creating an environment where everyone can enjoy responsible gambling without fear or uncertainty about fairness or transparency being compromised by any means whatsoever!

The Importance of Revenue Auditors in Regulatory Compliance

Revenue auditors in the casino industry have a critical role to play when it comes upholding regulatory compliance. They ensure that all operations align with various laws, standards and regulations governing gaming sectors. This section delves into their specific responsibilities and contributions towards maintaining adherence.

Auditing Internal Controls:

The importance of segregation in casino finance operations cannot be overstated. Revenue auditors ensure that no one person has unchecked control over critical financial processes, thus preventing potential fraud or mismanagement from occurring. This meticulous examination is crucial for maintaining transparency and trust within the industry.

Financial transactions require proper authorization protocols to ensure their legitimacy and compliance with regulatory requirements. Auditors assess these procedures for credit transactions, large payouts or other financial activities that may have implications on the company's overall performance. The establishment of clear protocols is essential in preventing fraudulent practices from occurring within an organization.

Monitoring Mechanisms: Regulatory compliance necessitates continuous monitoring of financial transactions. Revenue auditors evaluate the effectiveness of these mechanisms, such as real time alerts for suspicious activities to promptly address any potential irregularities.

Gaming Verification

The regulation of casino games ensures that they are conducted fairly and transparently. Revenue auditors investigate the mechanics behind each game verifying that odds accurately represent what is advertised while also adhering to regulatory standards. This process guarantees fairness for all players involved in gaming activities within a particular jurisdiction.

Auditors play a crucial role in ensuring that payouts are accurate and fair during gaming activities. They carefully examine the rules of each game to ensure winners receive their rightful earnings without any discrepancies or violations which could result in regulatory sanctions being imposed upon operators. This process helps maintain transparency within the industry while protecting both players' interests as well as those who run these games legally.

Gaming regulations impose specific rules for every type of game. Revenue auditors ensure that casinos adhere to these guidelines, guaranteeing a fair playing field and preventing any violations from occurring.

Regulatory Authorities Reporting

In the event that irregularities or potential compliance issues are identified during a revenue audit, its essential for professionals to prepare detailed reports promptly. This is crucial in maintaining transparency and trust with regulatory authorities by ensuring timely reporting.

Auditors play a critical role in ensuring that all documentation presented to regulatory bodies is accurate, complete and consistent with the information gathered during audits. This includes financial statements, transaction records as well as any other relevant documents pertaining to regulatory enquiries. It's imperative for auditors to ensure that every detail provided meets these standards so there are no discrepancies or inconsistencies when it comes time for review by authorities.

In order to address regulatory concerns revenue auditors may collaborate with legal teams. This entails providing necessary documentation and insights that support legal proceedings while demonstrating the casinos commitment towards compliance. Collaboration between these two departments is crucial in ensuring adherence to regulations while maintaining transparency within operations.

Collaborating with Regulatory Agencies

Revenue auditors must prioritize establishing and maintaining open lines of communication with regulatory agencies. This involves providing regular updates on findings as well as addressing any inquiries promptly to foster a collaborative relationship between both parties.

When regulatory authorities raise inquiries or requests for information revenue auditors play a crucial role in responding. Their ability to provide clear and comprehensive responses helps build trust with these entities while demonstrating the casinos commitment towards cooperation.

In summary revenue auditors play a critical role in maintaining regulatory compliance within the casino industry. Their detailed auditing procedures, comprehensive documentation practices and effective communication strategies all contribute to an environment of transparency and accountability that fosters positive relationships with regulators while ensuring legal adherence by casinos. This approach ultimately leads towards building trustworthy partnerships between stakeholder players including patrons who benefit from fair gaming experiences due to this diligent oversight process. Therefore, it is clear why these professionals are considered guardians of integrity within their field.

Ongoing Communication:

Regular updates are an essential component of revenue auditing in casinos. Auditors establish regular communication channels with regulatory agencies to provide information on financial operations, audit findings and any changes made within the internal controls system. This constant dialogue promotes transparency while also building a cooperative relationship between both parties involved. By keeping each other informed at all times both sides can work together towards achieving their goals more effectively than ever before!

Collaborating with regulatory authorities requires transparency in sharing audit findings. By openly communicating identified risks and areas for improvement casinos demonstrate their commitment to compliance while holding themselves accountable. This approach fosters trust among stakeholders who value honesty above all else.

How to Respond to Regulatory Inquiries

Regulatory authorities may pose inquiries seeking clarification or additional information from revenue auditors. These professionals play a crucial role in crafting timely and comprehensive responses that address each aspect of the inquiry with accuracy and transparency.

Auditors play a crucial role in ensuring that casinos adhere to regulatory requirements by providing supporting documentation. This may include financial statements, audit reports and other relevant records which serve as evidence of compliance with these rules. The provision of such information is essential for maintaining transparency within the industry while also protecting consumers from fraudulent practices.

Revenue auditors take a proactive stance when addressing potential issues or concerns raised by regulatory agencies. This involves anticipating upcoming requirements from these authorities and implementing necessary changes beforehand while also communicating with them about their actions preemptively. By doing so they are able to avoid any surprises down the line that could negatively impact their business operations.

When regulatory concerns arise during audit revenue auditors often collaborate with government agencies to conduct joint investigations. This approach allows both parties to contribute their expertise and uncover the root causes of issues while implementing corrective measures. The cooperative nature ensures that all bases are covered in finding solutions for any problems identified by these investigations. By working together effectively, everyone involved can achieve positive outcomes from this process.

Legal Compliance Support:

Collaborating with Legal Teams: Revenue auditors work closely alongside legal teams when dealing with regulatory issues that may have significant implications for their clients. They provide valuable insights, thorough analysis and comprehensive documentation to support the proceedings ensuring a cohesive approach towards addressing these concerns effectively. This collaboration helps ensure success in navigating complex legal landscapes while maintaining compliance standards set by governing bodies.

Regulatory changes can be challenging for casinos as they require adjustments in their operations. Revenue auditors work alongside legal teams to navigate these modifications and ensure that the establishment remains compliant with new regulations while implementing any necessary alterations promptly.

Trust Building and Maintenance

By working together effectively revenue auditors play a crucial role in maintaining the casinos reputation for transparency and accountability. This commitment to compliance also fosters trust with regulatory agencies leading to positive relationships between all parties involved.

Regular consultations are an integral part of revenue auditors' work. These interactions with regulatory authorities offer opportunities for industry best practices sharing, regulatory updates discussions and collaborative efforts aimed at enhancing overall compliance levels. Through these engagements both parties can benefit from each other's expertise while promoting a culture of transparency within the sector. Ultimately this leads to better outcomes for all stakeholders involved in regulated industries.

Collaborating with regulatory agencies is a constant endeavor for revenue auditors. Maintaining open communication channels promptly addressing inquiries and actively participating in joint efforts are crucial components of this process. Through these actions, auditors contribute to creating an environment that adheres to existing regulations while also preparing casinos for future changes. This collaboration ultimately ensures transparency within the industry as well as compliance with all applicable laws governing it.

Ethics in Regulatory Compliance

Revenue auditing within the casino industry requires strict adherence to ethical standards, particularly when it comes down to regulatory compliance. This section delves into how revenue auditors maintain integrity while also keeping confidentiality intact and conducting themselves responsibly in accordance with established rules and regulations.

Maintaining Integrity and Objectivity

Unbiased Auditing: Revenue auditors are committed to upholding the principles of integrity and objectivity throughout their work. They conduct thorough assessments with an unprejudiced mindset ensuring that all findings accurately reflect the casinos financial operations without any preconceived notions or biases influencing them in any way whatsoever. This is crucial for maintaining transparency within the industry while also providing accurate information for decision making purposes.

Auditing requires unwavering independence to maintain its integrity. Revenue auditors must make decisions and recommendations based solely on evidence rather than external pressures or influences. This level of objectivity ensures that their findings are trustworthy and reliable. Confidentiality and Data Security

As revenue auditors deal with highly sensitive financial information, they must uphold the highest standards of confidentiality. This means taking every precaution necessary to prevent unauthorized access or disclosure while handling this delicate data. Ethical considerations require that these professionals treat all such information with utmost care and respect.

Auditors implement secure document management practices to safeguard confidential information. This involves encryption, password protection and restricted access measures that ensure only authorized personnel have access to sensitive data. The implementation of these measures ensures the security of all documents under their care.

Balancing Transparency and Confidentiality: A Challenge for Businesses

Revenue auditors must navigate a delicate balance between transparency and confidentiality. Ethical considerations guide their decision-making process when determining the appropriate level of information sharing with regulatory authorities while still protecting sensitive data. This requires careful consideration to ensure compliance without compromising privacy or security concerns.

To ensure transparency and compliance with regulatory requirements ethical revenue auditors establish clear communication protocols when sharing information. This involves defining the scope of data being shared, outlining its purpose securely transmitting it while maintaining confidentiality at all times.

Ethical Conduct Training for Employees

Revenue auditors play a crucial role in fostering an ethical culture within casinos by promoting awareness and adherence to high standards of conduct. This involves providing training programs for staff members emphasizing the significance of upholding moral principles when handling financial operations. With their efforts, they help create a more responsible gaming environment that benefits both players and businesses alike.

Auditors face complex situations that require them to make ethical decisions. Ethics training equips casino employees with the tools necessary for recognizing and resolving these dilemmas effectively. This preparation enables auditors to navigate challenging scenarios confidently while upholding high standards of conduct. By prioritizing ethical decision making through comprehensive education programs, organizations can ensure their staff members are well prepared when faced with difficult choices on behalf of clients or stakeholders alike.

Ethical Collaboration in Regulatory Matters

Revenue auditors are expected to uphold ethical conduct in all interactions with regulatory authorities. This includes being honest and transparent when communicating information to these bodies ensuring that everything provided is accurate and complete.

Ethical auditors prioritize avoiding conflicts of interest that could compromise their ability to perform objective assessments. This entails disclosing any potential conflicts and implementing measures aimed at mitigating them from impacting the auditing process. By doing so they ensure fairness in all aspects of their work.

Continuous Ethical Oversight:

Casinos have taken steps to implement ethical review processes for revenue auditors. These assessments ensure that all auditors uphold high standards of conduct and identify areas where they can improve their performance. The goal is to maintain a fair playing field for everyone involved in the gaming industry.

Auditors who prioritize ethics stay up to date on evolving guidelines and standards within their profession. This continuous education enables them to navigate complex ethical challenges in an ever-changing regulatory environment with ease.

The importance of ethical considerations cannot be overstated when it comes to revenue auditors in the casino industry. By upholding principles such as integrity, confidentiality and responsible conduct during their work they contribute significantly towards maintaining regulatory compliance while also building trust with both internal stakeholders and external authorities alike. In summary: professionalism is key!

Improving Casino Revenue Auditing

Excellence is achieved through continuous improvement in any field including casino revenue auditing. This chapter delves into the principles and practices that enable revenue auditors to refine their methodologies stay current with industry advancements and contribute towards progressive audit processes.

By embracing these strategies, they can achieve greater success while ensuring long term growth within this dynamic sector.

Revenue auditors must possess adaptability as they navigate the ever-changing landscape of casino operations. In this section we explore how these professionals use innovative strategies to handle changes in technology, regulations and business dynamics. By staying flexible revenue auditors can remain effective even when faced with unexpected challenges or shifts within their industry.

Audit Approaches: Flexibility

Dynamic Regulatory Landscape: Revenue auditors understand that the regulatory environment for casinos is constantly evolving. From changes in gaming laws to modifications of reporting requirements and shifts in compliance standards - these alterations require constant vigilance from revenue auditors who must adjust their approach accordingly.

Technological advancements have transformed the casino industry in recent years. As a result, revenue auditors must be adaptable and flexible when it comes to incorporating new gaming technology into their strategies - whether its mobile platforms online games or innovative slot machine designs. Keeping up with these changes is crucial for ensuring fairness and accuracy in all aspects of casino operations.

Casinos are constantly evolving their business models to stay competitive in today's market. This could mean introducing new gaming formats or expanding into online platforms. Adaptive auditors understand this and tailor their methodologies accordingly so they can provide comprehensive coverage of the casino's financial landscape.

Risk-Based Auditing:

Revenue auditors are skilled at identifying key risks within casino operations by conducting comprehensive risk assessments. They evaluate the potential impact and likelihood of various threats to prioritize their efforts on addressing critical areas first. This approach ensures that resources are allocated effectively towards mitigating significant risks quickly and efficiently. The ability to identify these crucial issues is essential for maintaining a secure environment where customers can enjoy gaming responsibly without fear or worry about fraudulent activity taking place behind closed doors. With this level of expertise in play, revenue auditing plays an integral role in safeguarding both player safety as well as overall business success.

Auditors understand that risks are not static and require continuous reassessment to remain relevant in today's fast paced casino industry. By conducting dynamic risk assessments, they ensure their focus aligns with current threats while keeping up with changes in the business environment. This approach ensures auditor effectiveness as well as safety for all parties involved.

Adaptive auditors recognize that no two situations are alike and tailor their approach accordingly. By continually assessing risks throughout the process, they can adjust plans as needed to address any new or changing factors in play ensuring an effective response at all times. This adaptable strategy keeps them focused on what matters most: mitigating potential threats before they become major issues downstream.

Incorporating Emerging Trends:

Revenue auditors are constantly on the lookout for emerging trends within casino operations. They stay informed about innovative gaming technology advancements, changing consumer preferences and global economic factors that could impact revenue streams. By anticipating these developments beforehand, they can proactively adjust their strategies accordingly. This approach ensures maximum efficiency in managing finances effectively while minimizing risks associated with unforeseen events or changes in market conditions. It also enables them to make informed decisions based on accurate data analysis rather than guesswork or assumptions. Overall, this level of preparedness is essential when working in such a dynamic industry as casinos where success depends heavily on adaptability and agility.

Auditors are constantly evaluating industry benchmarks and best practices to remain ahead of emerging trends. By adopting proven methodologies from leading casinos while embracing innovative approaches auditors enhance the adaptability of their audit processes. This ensures that they stay up-to-date with current developments in the gaming sector.

In today's rapidly evolving technological landscape casino auditors must stay ahead of the curve by embracing new innovations. By incorporating cutting edge tools such as data analytics, artificial intelligence or blockchain technology into their workflows they can enhance efficiency and accuracy while also improving overall revenue potential within this dynamic industry sector. As these advancements become more widespread among competitors those who fail to adapt may find themselves left behind in an increasingly competitive marketplace where success depends on being able to keep up with constant change.

For the rapidly evolving casino industry adaptive audit strategies are essential for revenue auditors. By adopting flexible approaches prioritizing risks and proactively incorporating emerging trends these professionals contribute significantly towards enhancing their methodologies' effectiveness in conducting successful audits of casinos' revenues. Ultimately this results in improved overall performance within the sector as a whole.

Technology Integration for Efficiency

In the fast-paced casino industry revenue auditors must stay ahead of the curve by leveraging technological advancements. This section explores how these professionals use cutting edge tools to streamline their operations and remain competitive in an ever-evolving landscape. With constant innovation driving change within this sector its essential for those involved with auditing processes to embrace technology as a means towards greater efficiency accuracy and overall effectiveness.

Automation of Routine Tasks

Data entry and validation are critical components of any revenue audit. Automation tools can streamline these processes by minimizing errors caused by manual input while also ensuring that the information being entered is accurate and reliable through data validation checks. This approach helps to expedite auditing tasks without compromising on quality or accuracy. By leveraging automated solutions for routine data entry activities, companies can reduce risks associated with human error while improving overall efficiency levels across their operations.

Modern audit software provides a comprehensive solution for generating reports that are both detailed and customizable. Auditors can tailor these documents to highlight key findings, anomalies or areas requiring attention without sacrificing accuracy. Automation in report generation ensures timely dissemination of results among relevant stakeholders. This feature is particularly useful when time constraints exist during the auditing process. Overall modern audit technology has significantly improved efficiency by streamlining reporting procedures while maintaining high standards of quality control.

Exception Tracking: Automated exception tracking tools are a boon for auditors as they help identify irregularities or deviations from established norms. By setting parameters for acceptable variations, these tools enable auditors to focus their attention on transactions or activities that fall outside predefined thresholds - streamlining the entire process of conducting an audit. With such automation in place, auditing becomes more efficient and effective than ever before!

Data Analytics for Insights:

Revenue auditors leverage sophisticated data analytics tools to gain deeper insights into financial transactions. These advanced algorithms and statistical analyses enable them to identify patterns, trends, and anomalies within large datasets quickly and accurately. This allows for efficient extraction of meaningful information that would otherwise be difficult or time consuming to obtain manually. With these powerful resources at their disposal revenue auditors are able to make informed decisions with greater confidence than ever before.

Auditors can leverage data analytics to identify revenue trends over time. By analyzing historical information, they gain insights into customer behavior, gaming preferences and non-gaming income streams that inform their decision-making process while also aiding in proactive audit planning. This approach ensures accuracy when assessing financial performance across different periods of operation.

Today's digital age casino operations face significant challenges when it comes to fraud detection. However, with the help of advanced technology such as sophisticated algorithms and artificial intelligence auditors can stay ahead of potential threats by analyzing transaction patterns for unusual behavior that may indicate fraudulent activity. This approach not only improves accuracy but also speeds up response times significantly - making it an essential tool in maintaining a secure gaming environment.

CASINO REVENUE AUDITING

Continuous Monitoring:

Technology has revolutionized the way casinos manage their finances by providing real time transaction tracking capabilities. With this technology auditors can keep a close eye on revenue streams and quickly identify any irregularities that may arise in order to take immediate action before they become bigger problems down the line. This constant monitoring helps ensure financial integrity within the establishment while also promoting transparency for all parties involved.

Automated alert systems play a crucial role in ensuring that auditors are notified of any unusual activities or deviations from established benchmarks. These early warning mechanisms allow for prompt investigation into potential issues before they escalate further down the line. By implementing such an approach through automation, audit teams can adopt proactive and responsive strategies when it comes to managing risk within their organizations.

Artificial Intelligence in Auditing Processes

Revenue auditors are now utilizing the power of predictive analytics fueled by artificial intelligence to anticipate future revenue trends. By analyzing historical data and identifying patterns AI algorithms provide valuable insights into potential fluctuations in revenue streams as well as areas that require attention. With this information at their fingertips auditors can make informed decisions about how best to manage finances moving forward.

Natural language processing (NLP) technologies have revolutionized the way auditors analyze spoken and written interactions within casinos. By analyzing customer feedback, employee communications, and textual data they gain nuanced insights into operational dynamics that may need improvement. This technology has become an essential tool for those who want to stay ahead of the game in today's competitive gaming industry.

The use of machine learning algorithms in fraud prevention has become increasingly popular among revenue auditors. These sophisticated systems continuously learn and adapt to new patterns of behavior allowing them to detect emerging forms of fraudulent activity with greater accuracy than ever before. With this technology at their disposal, auditors are better equipped than ever before when it comes to keeping businesses safe from harmful financial crimes.

Cybersecurity Measures in Revenue Auditing

The digital age has brought about significant changes in the way auditors conduct their work. One of these is through cloud-based solutions that offer convenience and efficiency but also require robust cybersecurity measures to protect sensitive financial data from unauthorized access or breaches. Audit teams ensure that such platforms implement strong encryption protocols alongside secure access controls so as not compromise on security while using them for revenue auditing processes.

To safeguard against cyber threats auditors, prioritize endpoint security measures. These precautions involve securing individual devices and endpoints within the casinos network to prevent unauthorized access and potential data breaches. This is crucial in ensuring that sensitive information remains protected at all times.

To ensure the integrity of their digital infrastructure casinos conduct regular security audits in collaboration with IT professionals. This technology driven assessments identify vulnerabilities and implement necessary patches to keep up with evolving cyber threats. By working together both parties can maintain a resilient system that keeps sensitive information safe from harm.

The integration of technology into revenue auditing represents a significant shift in the way things are done. By embracing automation, data analytics and artificial intelligence alongside robust cybersecurity measures; auditors have found themselves empowered with greater efficiency and precision when navigating through complex casino industry scenarios. This approach ensures continuous improvement within their methodologies as they continue to adapt to changing circumstances over time. The benefits that come from leveraging these technological advancements cannot be ignored - it is clear why many see this move towards digitalization as an essential step forward for any organization looking to stay competitive today.

Professional Development and Training

CASINO REVENUE AUDITING

The success of casino revenue auditing depends on the continuous development and training of its professionals. This section delves into how auditors proactively stay up to date with regulatory changes, technological advancements, and industry best practices in order to maintain excellence within their field. By prioritizing these measures, they are able to ensure that they remain at the forefront of innovation while also upholding high standards for accuracy and accountability.

Regulatory Changes - Stay Informed

Staying abreast of regulatory changes is essential for revenue auditors operating in the gaming industry. They prioritize subscribing to regular updates from local, national and international sources while actively participating in seminars and forums where these matters are discussed at length. By doing so they remain informed about any potential impacts on their work or clients' operations. This approach ensures that all parties involved adhere strictly to legal requirements while minimizing risks associated with non-compliance.

Professional development for revenue auditors involves honing their skills in interpreting and implementing new regulations effectively. This requires an investment of time into understanding the nuances of freshly introduced laws ensuring that audit methodologies align with updated compliance standards. By doing so, they are able capable professionals who can navigate complex legal frameworks successfully.

Emerging Technologies Training

As technology continues to evolve rapidly within the casino industry revenue auditors are constantly engaged in workshops and webinars focused on emerging technologies. These sessions provide valuable hands-on experiences as well as insights into practical applications of cutting-edge technologies such as blockchain, artificial intelligence or data analytics. By staying up to date with these developments through continuous learning opportunities like this professionals can remain competitive while also ensuring they're providing accurate assessments for their clients.

Revenue auditors work closely with IT specialists to gain insight into technological advancements. This collaboration enables knowledge transfer and ensures that auditors are well versed in the intricacies of IT systems, cybersecurity measures, and digital innovations. By collaborating effectively, they can stay up-to-date on emerging trends while also enhancing their expertise within this field.

Auditing certifications are a popular choice among revenue auditors who seek to validate their expertise and enhance their knowledge base. Professional designations such as Certified Internal Auditor (CIA) or Certified Information Systems Auditor (CISA provide structure for ongoing learning while also showcasing one's proficiency in this field of work.

To enhance their expertise in casino revenue auditing, many professionals pursue specialized certifications focused on gaming-specific procedures. These programs cover topics such as regulatory frameworks governing the industry along with internal control mechanisms and compliance requirements unique to this sector. By obtaining these credentials individuals demonstrate a deep understanding of how best practices can be applied within casinos for optimal results.

Collaborative Learning and Knowledge Sharing

Revenue auditors play an integral role in ensuring that their organizations operate within legal boundaries. To achieve this goal, they actively participate in internal training programs covering various topics such as audit methodologies, regulatory updates and best practices. These sessions create a collaborative learning environment among colleagues fostering growth and development for all involved parties. The result is better performance outcomes which ultimately benefit both employees and stakeholders alike.

Cross training initiatives are a crucial aspect of an auditor's education within the casino environment. By exposing themselves to various aspects such as gaming revenue, non-gaming income streams and compliance regulations they can develop versatile skills that will serve them well in their careers ahead. This approach ensures that auditors have all bases covered when it comes time for assessments or evaluations. The benefits include improved efficiency at work while also being able to handle any unexpected situations with ease due to having had prior experience handling similar scenarios beforehand through cross training programs.

CASINO REVENUE AUDITING

Industry Conference Attendance

Networking and Knowledge Exchange: Revenue auditors are constantly attending industry conferences and conventions to expand their knowledge base. These events offer opportunities for networking with peers, exchanging experiences and gaining insights into emerging trends within the casino sector. By participating in these gatherings' revenue auditors can broaden their understanding of this dynamic field.

Exposure to Thought Leaders: Industry conferences provide opportunities for revenue auditors to gain insight from experts and thought leaders in the field of casino management, gaming technologies, and regulatory compliance. These sessions are highly sought after by professionals who want access to cutting edge knowledge that can help them stay ahead of their competition. Online Learning Platforms - Utilization

Online learning platforms have become increasingly popular among revenue auditors who are looking to expand their knowledge base. E-learning modules provide a flexible and accessible way for these professionals to stay up to date with relevant topics such as audit techniques, regulatory updates or technological advancements without having to physically attend classes in person. With this approach they can learn at anytime from anywhere - making it easier than ever before!

Revenue auditing requires a deep understanding of complex financial concepts and procedures. Web based training courses offer an accessible solution for busy professionals who want to expand their knowledge without leaving the comforts of home or office space. These tailored programs provide detailed instructional materials along with interactive exercises that reinforce learning outcomes effectively. With this approach learners can acquire new skills at anytime from anywhere in the world!

The commitment to excellence is an integral part of being a revenue auditor. This requires continuous professional development and training in order for them stay informed about regulatory changes while embracing emerging technologies that are relevant for their work environment. Additionally, obtaining certifications along with collaborative learning opportunities such as attending industry conferences helps keep the skill set current so they can meet evolving demands within casino revenue auditing effectively. Therefore, its essential for all revenue auditors who want success in this field to prioritize these activities regularly if they wish to remain competitive over time.

Feedback Mechanisms and Process Evaluation

Achieving continuous improvement in casino revenue auditing requires a comprehensive system of feedback mechanisms and rigorous process evaluation. This section delves into how revenue auditors actively seek out feedback through post-audit reviews while implementing thorough evaluations to refine their methodologies for more effective results.

Reflective analysis is an integral part of revenue auditing. After completing each audit, experts engage in comprehensive post-audit reviews that involve analyzing the entire process from start to finish. This includes examining what went well during the audit and identifying any challenges encountered along the way while assessing its overall effectiveness. Through this reflective approach, revenue auditors are able better understand how they can improve future audits for maximum efficiency and accuracy.

Post audit reviews are an essential tool for identifying areas that could benefit from enhancements. Auditors evaluate whether or not the set objectives were achieved and assess any deviations in approach as well as unexpected challenges encountered during the process. This information is crucial when making decisions about future improvements within organizations.

Feedback from Stakeholders:

Revenue auditors prioritize engaging with casino management to ensure that their work aligns with expectations and requirements. This feedback loop enables them to gain valuable insights into how findings are utilized for decision making purposes as well as operational enhancements within the organization. The active involvement of both parties ensures a seamless process while also promoting transparency throughout all levels of leadership within the establishment. By working together towards common goals, revenue auditing becomes more effective in identifying areas where improvements can be made which ultimately leads to better outcomes overall.

Auditors present their findings to relevant stakeholders after conducting audits. This entails collaborative discussions with finance teams, compliance officers and operational managers among others. The open communication channels enable feedback exchange which helps address concerns raised by these parties while clarifying any points of contention that may arise during the process. Auditors prioritize transparency in this regard as it ensures accuracy and effectiveness throughout every stage of an auditing project.

Post audit reviews and stakeholder feedback provide valuable insights that can be used to implement lessons learned. Auditors leverage this knowledge by refining their methodologies updating procedures and incorporating improvements aimed at enhancing future audits' efficiency and effectiveness. The end result is a more streamlined process with better outcomes for all involved parties.

Audit plans are subject to constant refinement based on feedback mechanisms. Successful auditing strategies that prove effective in one instance can be integrated into standard operating procedures for future use while challenges identified during an audit require mitigation measures before they become problematic again later down the line. The goal is always to improve upon previous efforts by making adjustments as needed so that each subsequent audit runs more smoothly than its predecessor did.

Industry Benchmarking

Regularly benchmarking against industry standards is a crucial aspect of revenue auditing. Auditors actively engage in this process by comparing their methodologies, processes and outcomes with recognized benchmarks within the casino audit sphere. Benchmarking helps identify areas where they can align or surpass best practices set forth by other professionals within the field. By doing so regularly auditors are able to stay up-to-date on current trends while continuously improving upon their own methods for conducting thorough yet efficient audits that benefit both themselves as well as those who rely on them for accurate financial reporting.

Benchmarking provides auditors with the opportunity to incorporate best practices identified through industry comparisons. This continuous integration of proven methodologies helps refine and optimize audit processes ensuring that they remain at the forefront of industry standards. The result is an enhanced level of quality in their work which ultimately benefits all parties involved.

Proven Methodologies Adoption

Revenue auditors are keen observers of success stories within their organization and beyond. They carefully study instances where audits resulted in positive outcomes to gain valuable insights into effective methodologies. These triumphs serve as benchmarks for future endeavors. By learning from these victories revenue auditors can improve the quality of their work and achieve greater results over time.

Auditors employ proven methodologies to identify effective strategies that they actively apply in their work. These may involve refining risk-based audit approaches, enhancing data analytics techniques or improving collaboration with other departments but ultimately all aim at driving continuous improvement within the organization. By doing so auditors ensure that their efforts are always aligned towards achieving optimal results for stakeholders involved.

New Technology Evaluation

Audit Processes and New Technologies: Revenue auditors understand the importance of testing new technologies before incorporating them into their routine practices. Pilot tests allow for controlled evaluations that help identify potential challenges while also providing valuable insights on how well these innovative tools work in real world scenarios. With this information at hand revenue auditors can make informed decisions about which technological advancements are worth investing time and resources into further development within their respective industries.

Collaboration with IT specialists is crucial when assessing new technologies. Auditors actively seek feedback from these professionals regarding compatibility, security and usability of audit technology under consideration. This collaborative approach ensures that any integration into the workflow runs smoothly without disruptions or complications. By working together towards a common goal - successful implementation - both parties benefit greatly in terms of efficiency gains and overall satisfaction levels.

The revenue auditor's commitment to excellence is underpinned by two key components: feedback mechanisms and continuous process evaluation. By actively seeking input from stakeholders engaging in post-audit reviews implementing lessons learned benchmarking against industry standards adopting proven methodologies evaluating new technologies - all while keeping an eye on the ever-changing needs of casinos - these professionals ensure that their practices remain dynamic responsive and effective over time. In summary? Feedback and evaluation are essential tools for maintaining high quality work within this field.

Best Practices Implementation

In casino revenue auditing continuous improvement is achieved through the adoption and application of industry best practices. This section explores how dedicated revenue auditors embrace these standards to enhance their processes' effectiveness, efficiency, and overall quality. By adopting a commitment towards excellence, they are able ensuring that every aspect of their work meets or exceeds expectations.

Adopting Proven Methodologies

Revenue auditors are meticulous in their analysis of successful audits within both their organization and the broader industry. By identifying key factors that contributed to these successes they gain valuable insights into proven methodologies which can be applied towards enhancing their own audit processes. Through this process revenue auditors continually refine their approach ensuring optimal results for all parties involved.

The adoption of proven methodologies has enabled revenue auditors to identify successful strategies that are now actively integrated into their standard operating procedures. This integration results in enhanced efficiency, accuracy and comprehensiveness within the audit process. The incorporation ensures optimal performance from these professionals who strive for excellence at all times.

Audit Procedures - Continuous Refinement

Post-Audit Evaluations: The revenue auditors conduct thorough post-audit evaluations after every audit. These assessments involve a comprehensive review of the auditing procedures used, identifying areas for improvement and formulating strategies to refine future audits based on lessons learned from previous experiences. This process ensures that all aspects are examined thoroughly before finalizing any results or recommendations.

Audit procedures are not static but rather subject to continuous refinement through iterative enhancements. Auditors actively seek opportunities for fine tuning their methodologies in order to ensure that each audit benefits from the cumulative knowledge gained through ongoing assessments. This approach ensures that every aspect of an audit's quality is optimized and improved upon over time.

Risk-Based Audit Approaches:

Dynamic Risk Assessments: Revenue auditors utilize dynamic risk assessment techniques to identify and prioritize potential risks within casino operations. By remaining adaptable in response to changes in the business environment these professionals ensure that their risk-based auditing approaches remain relevant and effective at all times.

Risk-based approaches enable auditors to allocate resources effectively. By focusing on areas of higher risk they optimize the use of time and resources enhancing both efficiency and impact in their audit procedures. This approach ensures that all aspects are covered thoroughly while minimizing wasteful expenditure. It ultimately leads to better results for everyone involved with fewer surprises along the way.

Utilization of Technology:

Revenue auditors rely on advanced tools and technologies to optimize their workflows. Automation, data analytics, and artificial intelligence are integrated into the process for greater efficiency, accuracy, and depth in audit procedures. This approach ensures that every aspect of revenue collection is thoroughly examined with precision.

Regular Technology Assessments: Auditors regularly assess technology solutions to ensure they remain aligned with industry best practices. This includes evaluating the security, functionality and relevance of audit technologies in order to maintain a cutting edge and effective auditing infrastructure.

Employee Training and Skill Development:

Revenue auditors understand the importance of continuous learning and development for themselves as well as their teams. They invest in training programs, workshops, and certifications that enhance audit skills while keeping up with industry trends and adapting to changing regulatory requirements. This commitment ensures they remain at the forefront of revenue management best practices.

Audit teams that prioritize cross training initiatives are better equipped to handle the complexities of casino revenue auditing. By fostering versatility and comprehensive understanding among team members, these programs promote a holistic approach that enables them to tackle diverse challenges presented by casinos operations effectively. Investing in such initiatives is therefore crucial for any organization looking to optimize its auditing processes.

Collaborative Learning and Knowledge Sharing

Revenue auditors prioritize active participation in industry networks, forums and conferences as a means of sharing knowledge and insights with peers. This collaborative approach enables them to refine their procedures continuously through ongoing learning opportunities provided by these events. The benefits are numerous - from staying up-to-date on emerging trends within the field to fostering valuable relationships that can lead to future partnerships or career advancement prospects. Ultimately this commitment helps ensure revenue auditing remains at its best possible standard.

Auditors play a critical role in contributing to internal knowledge repositories that enable the sharing of best practices, successful strategies and valuable insights within their team. These resources serve as an essential reference point for auditors looking to enhance their own practice based on collective expertise. The benefits are twofold - not only do they gain access to this wealth of information but also contribute towards its growth by adding new ideas or perspectives. This collaborative approach ensures continuous improvement while fostering a culture of learning among colleagues. Ultimately it results in better outcomes for all parties involved.

Revenue auditors who prioritize continuous improvement understand that implementing best practices is an ongoing process. To achieve this goal, they benchmark against industry standards adopt proven methodologies refine their auditing procedures employ risk-based approaches leverage technology and foster collaborative learning environments for employees. These efforts contribute to the evolution of effective casino revenue auditing practices over time. By embracing these strategies auditors can ensure they remain at the forefront of innovation within their field.

QA and Compliance Oversight - Ensuring Quality

The integrity of casino revenue auditing is crucial for maintaining public trust and adherence to regulatory requirements. This chapter examines the mechanisms employed by revenue auditors in ensuring that their processes are accurate, reliable, and compliant with all relevant laws.

Regular Methodology Evaluations: Revenue auditors undertake periodic assessments of their audit methodologies. These evaluations involve a comprehensive review of all aspects of the process from identifying risks to generating reports ensuring that they align with industry standards and regulatory requirements. This approach helps ensure accuracy in reporting while maintaining compliance with legal obligations.

Internal quality assurance incorporates continuous improvement feedback loops that enable auditors to actively seek input from team members regarding the effectiveness of their methodologies. This approach allows for iterative enhancements based on practical insights and experiences gained through collaboration with colleagues. By doing so, internal quality assurance becomes more efficient over time as it adapts to changing circumstances while remaining focused on delivering high-quality results.

Peer Reviews and Cross-Verification:

Peer Evaluation Processes: Internal quality assurance involves peer reviews where auditors within the team evaluate each other's work. This collaborative approach helps identify potential blind spots ensures consistency in audit approaches and promotes a culture of accountability among team members. By working together towards common goals through this process everyone benefits from improved performance outcomes.

Auditors implement cross verification protocols to ensure the accuracy of audit findings. This involves comparing results with historical trends and verifying calculations for enhanced reliability and precision in audit outcomes. The implementation of these measures is crucial as it ensures that all parties involved can trust the data presented by an auditor.

Gaming Regulation Compliance

Revenue auditors are required to undergo regular training sessions that keep them up-to-date with any changes in gaming regulations. The importance of compliance cannot be overstated as these professionals ensure their methodologies align perfectly with the specific rules governing casino operations. By doing so they maintain a high level of accuracy and precision when conducting revenue audits. This approach ensures fairness for all parties involved while also protecting against fraudulent activities within this industry sector.

Auditors prioritize engaging with regulatory authorities to gain a comprehensive understanding of the standards and requirements set forth by these entities. This proactive approach enables auditors to foster positive relationships while ensuring that they are fully compliant with all necessary regulations. By actively seeking clarification from regulators on their expectations, auditors can confidently navigate complex legal landscapes without fear or uncertainty.

AML Compliance

To ensure compliance with AML regulations revenue auditors integrate relevant protocols into their audit processes. This involves reviewing customer transactions and monitoring for suspicious activities while ensuring that casinos financial operations align with reporting requirements. By doing so they help prevent money laundering and other illicit practices in the gaming industry.

Auditors and AML compliance officers within casinos work together closely to ensure comprehensive regulatory compliance. Through this collaboration auditors provide valuable insights into financial transactions that may require further scrutiny from a compliance perspective. This approach ensures an all-encompassing strategy towards meeting legal requirements while maintaining transparency in operations.

Independent Audits and Third-Party Assessments

To ensure that revenue audits remain objective and transparent periodic external auditing is required. This involves bringing in independent audit firms or outside experts who will review the methodologies, procedures and outcomes of these audits with an unbiased eye. By doing so it ensures that any potential issues are identified early on and addressed accordingly.

To ensure the accuracy and reliability of casino revenue auditing processes, some auditors may engage third-party experts for assessments. These evaluations measure internal control effectiveness as well as regulatory compliance while also appraising overall quality in audit procedures. By utilizing external expertise through these assessments, auditors can strengthen their ability to detect potential errors or discrepancies within financial records.

Continuous Stakeholder Monitoring and Feedback

Real-Time Monitoring Systems:

Real time monitoring is an essential tool used by revenue auditors in casinos. This system allows for constant tracking of financial transactions and immediate detection of any irregularities that may arise. By proactively addressing these issues before they become larger problems the integrity of finances remains intact. The implementation of real time monitoring systems ensures a seamless operation with minimal risk of fraud or other forms of misconduct within the gaming industry.

Auditors prioritize stakeholder feedback for continuous improvement by actively seeking input from casino management, regulatory authorities and other relevant parties. By engaging with these groups' auditors gather valuable insights that enable them to address concerns while implementing improvements in their methodologies. This approach ensures the highest level of quality control throughout every aspect of gaming operations.

Auditing Processes and Stakeholder Involvement

Revenue auditors prioritize transparency in their communication with stakeholders throughout the auditing process. This entails keeping them informed through regular updates on preliminary findings and progress reports until final outcomes are reached. The goal is to ensure that everyone involved remains well-informed at all times.

When faced with complex challenges or discrepancies auditors prioritize collaboration over confrontation. By working together with stakeholders, they create an environment that fosters cooperation and shared commitment towards regulatory compliance and financial transparency. This approach ensures that all parties are invested in finding solutions rather than assigning blame.

Continuous Training and Professional Development

Training on Evolving Regulations

Adaptive training programs are essential for revenue auditors who need to stay ahead of changing gaming regulations. These courses provide a comprehensive understanding of the regulatory landscape and equip professionals with skills necessary for navigating any changes in compliance standards. By participating in these adaptive programs, auditors can remain at the forefront of their field while ensuring that they meet all legal requirements.

Auditors need to stay up-to-date with compliance requirements in order to conduct accurate audits. Integrating these updates into training initiatives ensures that they have the latest knowledge at their fingertips when assessing companies' financial statements or other records. This integration allows for more effective and efficient auditing processes overall.

Emerging Technologies Training:

Staying ahead of the curve is crucial for revenue auditors working in casino operations. Achieving this goal, they participate regularly in technology focused workshops that cover topics such as blockchain applications, artificial intelligence and data analytics. These sessions enable them to evaluate accurately how these emerging technologies impact their bottom line. By staying informed about new developments through continuous learning opportunities like these workshops; auditors are better equipped than ever before when it comes time assess revenue streams effectively.

Collaboration with IT Specialists: Auditors work closely alongside IT professionals to ensure that their training initiatives align with technological advancements. By actively seeking insights from these experts' auditors are able to create programs that effectively address the evolving landscape of technology. This collaboration is crucial for ensuring success in today's rapidly changing world where digitalization plays an increasingly important role.

The integration of quality assurance practices, compliance oversight, external audits, continuous monitoring and stakeholder involvement alongside ongoing training all contribute to the overall effectiveness and credibility of casino revenue auditing processes. Revenue auditors remain committed to upholding unwaveringly high standards for accuracy, integrity and regulatory compliance in this dynamic industry.

Ethical Issues in Casino Revenue Auditing

Ethical principles are essential for maintaining transparency, integrity and trust in financial processes within casino revenue auditing. In this chapter we explore the ethical standards that guide revenue auditors throughout their work while also examining how these guidelines are upheld during each stage of an audit. By adhering to high moral values at all times those involved can ensure fairness and accuracy when dealing with sensitive information related to finances.

Ethical Code for Revenue Auditors

Professional Integrity Commitment

Revenue auditors adhere to a comprehensive code of ethics that outlines principles for professional conduct. This code emphasizes integrity, objectivity, confidentiality and competence as core tenets guiding their roles. The importance placed on these values underscores the significance of maintaining high standards in all aspects of revenue auditing work.

When confronted with complex situations auditors rely on an ethical decision-making framework. This involves a systematic approach that considers potential impacts on stakeholders while adhering to established principles of morality and integrity. By utilizing this methodology auditors are able make informed decisions based upon sound reasoning rather than impulse or emotion.

Independence and Objectivity

Casino revenue auditors are required to maintain a level of independence from operational and financial management within the establishment. This separation ensures that all assessments conducted by these professionals remain objective, free from undue influence or bias towards any particular outcome. The importance placed on this requirement highlights how critical it is for casinos to have reliable information when making important decisions about their operations.

Auditors take proactive steps to avoid conflicts of interest that could compromise their independence. This involves disclosing any personal or financial relationships that may impact objectivity and implementing appropriate measures to address potential issues. By doing so they maintain an unbiased approach towards auditing activities.

Audit Process Objectivity

Auditors are committed to maintaining objectivity in their assessments by basing conclusions on evidence, facts and professional judgment. They avoid being influenced by personal biases or external pressures that could compromise the integrity of an audit process. This commitment ensures fairness and accuracy throughout every stage of evaluation.

CASINO REVENUE AUDITING

Auditors prioritize transparency and clarity when reporting audit findings. They present objective assessments that distinguish between facts and interpretations while providing stakeholders with a comprehensive understanding of the outcomes. This approach ensures all parties are informed about what was found during an audit's investigation.

Protecting sensitive financial and operational information is paramount for revenue auditors. They adhere to strict protocols that ensure confidentiality throughout the entire process of conducting an audit while handling storing transmitting or accessing such data. This approach ensures maximum protection against any unauthorized access attempts by third parties who may seek to exploit this valuable information.

Auditors have the responsibility of carefully selecting who receives information from their audit findings. This measure helps safeguard sensitive data and prevent unauthorized access or dissemination. The limited disclosure ensures that only authorized individuals are privy to this confidential information.

Auditors implement secure information systems to protect sensitive data from unauthorized access and maintain its integrity. This involves implementing encryption protocols, access controls, as well as conducting regular security assessments that identify potential vulnerabilities for improvement. By doing so they ensure the protection of valuable information assets against any threats or risks posed by cybercriminals.

Revenue auditors play a critical role in ensuring compliance with privacy regulations governing the collection and handling of personal and financial data. This includes adherence to strict industry standards aimed at protecting individuals' private information from unauthorized access or disclosure. The revenue auditor is responsible for enforcing these laws by implementing measures that safeguard sensitive information while still allowing businesses to operate efficiently within legal boundaries. By doing so they help maintain trust between consumers and companies alike.

Professional Skepticism and Due Professional Care

Professional Skepticism:

Auditors are trained to approach evidence with a critical eye through professional skepticism. This means maintaining an inquisitive mindset while evaluating data and seeking additional corroboration when necessary for accurate audit findings.

Professional skepticism encourages auditors to conduct comprehensive inquiries and verifications. This approach enables them to detect potential fraud or irregularities, promoting a proactive stance towards identifying discrepancies. The thoroughness of this process ensures that no stone is left unturned when it comes to maintaining transparency within financial records.

Due Professional Care:

Auditors demonstrate their due professional care by implementing comprehensive audit procedures. This involves meticulously planning and conducting fieldwork while documenting every step of the process to showcase their thoroughness and diligence in work. The result is a transparent representation of how they approach each task with precision and attention to detail.

Auditors recognize the importance of continuous professional development as a means to enhance their skills and knowledge. By prioritizing this commitment, they ensure that they are well equipped for any emerging challenges or changes in regulatory landscapes. This dedication ensures auditor excellence at all times.

Clear and Effective Communication

Auditors prioritize clear and effective communication with stakeholders throughout the auditing process. This entails offering regular updates on progress made during each stage of assessment while also clarifying objectives set forth by both parties involved in this endeavor. Additionally, they ensure that all relevant individuals understand what is being assessed along with its purpose as well as outcomes achieved upon completion. Such efforts are critical for maintaining transparency within any organization or business venture undergoing an audit evaluation.

Timely reporting is a critical aspect of maintaining transparency during audits. Auditors prioritize presenting their findings promptly so that stakeholders can make informed decisions based on the outcomes without any unnecessary delays. This approach ensures efficiency and effectiveness in managing risks while also enhancing accountability within an organization or company.

Auditors prioritize transparency by disclosing any limitations in their auditing procedures. This involves communicating constraints such as restricted access to information that may impact the comprehensiveness of an audit's findings.

Auditors prioritize fostering an open dialogue with stakeholders by encouraging questions and discussions about audit findings. This collaborative approach promotes transparency while ensuring that all parties have the opportunity to seek clarification or provide additional insights. By doing so, auditors create a more comprehensive understanding of their work's impact on those involved in its execution.

The foundation of casino revenue auditing lies in ethical considerations that guide auditors towards maintaining professional integrity, safeguarding confidentiality while exercising skepticism and communicating transparently. Adherence to these principles ensures credibility within the complex landscape of gaming operations by fostering trust among stakeholders involved with this industry.

Casino Revenue Auditing - Trends and Future Directions

The world of casino revenue auditing is constantly evolving due to technological advancements, regulatory changes and shifting industry dynamics. In this chapter we explore emerging trends that are influencing the future direction of casino revenue auditing.

Technological Advancements

The integration of blockchain technology has opened up new possibilities for enhancing transparency in financial transactions. Casinos are exploring how this decentralized ledger can be used to improve accuracy and traceability while also ensuring that all revenue is recorded accurately on a transparent platform. This could revolutionize the way we think about gaming operations as well as other industries where trustworthiness matters most. With such advancements at hand, it seems like only good things lie ahead!

Audit processes are set to undergo a transformation with the introduction of smart contracts. These self-executing agreements written directly into code have potential for automating certain aspects of auditing operations while enhancing efficiency and compliance standards. With payment verification streamlined through this technology it could lead to significant improvements in overall performance within financial institutions. As such its worth considering how incorporating these innovative tools can benefit your organization.

Artificial Intelligence and Machine Learning

The use of AI and machine learning algorithms has revolutionized the field of predictive analytics. Revenue auditors are now leveraging these technologies to forecast revenue trends identify anomalies proactively address potential financial irregularities with greater accuracy than ever before possible. This cutting-edge approach is transforming how businesses operate by providing valuable insights into future performance that were previously unattainable through traditional methods alone. With this powerful tool at their disposal companies can make informed decisions about investments strategic partnerships or other key initiatives with confidence in knowing they have a clear understanding of what lies ahead for them financially speaking.

Machine learning algorithms have revolutionized fraud detection by continuously adapting to new patterns of fraudulent activities. Revenue auditors leverage this technology for real time monitoring and prevention of fraudulent transactions. With its ability to quickly identify potential threats machine learning has become an essential tool in combating financial crimes.

Enhanced Data Analytics

Big Data Analytics:

The use of big data analytics has revolutionized the way revenue auditors approach their work. By analyzing vast datasets comprehensively, they can identify trends in customer behavior and potential areas for concern with greater accuracy than ever before. This nuanced understanding allows them to gain a deeper insight into casino operations. The result? Better decision making based on more informed insights. It is no wonder why this technology is becoming increasingly popular among those who want better results from their gaming businesses!

Real time data processing is made possible through advanced analytics tools that enable auditors to monitor financial transactions as they occur. This capability enhances the agility of revenue auditors by allowing for immediate responses to emerging issues and anomalies in real-time. With this technology at their fingertips, auditors can stay ahead of potential problems before they become major concerns.

Risk Management with Predictive Analytics

Proactive Risk Identification: Predictive analytics models are utilized for proactive risk identification. By analyzing historical data and patterns revenue auditors can anticipate potential risks and allocate resources strategically to address high-risk areas before issues arise. This approach ensures that problems do not go unnoticed until they become major concerns. With this strategy in place companies have a better chance of avoiding costly mistakes or missed opportunities.

Predictive analytics has become an integral part of risk-based audit approaches. By utilizing predictive models, auditors can assess the likelihood of specific risks materializing and allocate their resources more effectively for a focused approach to tackling these challenges head on. This integration provides significant benefits in terms of efficiency and accuracy when it comes to identifying potential issues before they escalate into major problems. With this technology at hand, businesses are better equipped than ever before to manage

CASINO REVENUE AUDITING

their operations with greater confidence knowing that any potential threats will be identified early enough for them to take action before anything serious happens.

Regulatory Technology (RegTech)

Regulatory compliance is a critical aspect of gaming operations. RegTech platforms have emerged as powerful tools for automating monitoring processes and ensuring adherence to complex regulations. Revenue auditors leverage these technologies in their work streamlining tasks while reducing risks associated with non-compliance violations.

RegTech solutions offer real time compliance reporting capabilities that benefit revenue auditors. Automated mechanisms provide instant insights into the casinos adherence to regulations allowing for prompt corrective actions and reducing regulatory risks. With this technology at their disposal auditors can stay on top of any potential issues before they become major problems.

Regulatory Reporting and Blockchain

Regulatory reporting is enhanced through blockchains immutability. By recording regulatory information on a blockchain auditors create an unalterable and transparent record of compliance that bolsters the credibility of their reports. This innovative approach to regulation ensures transparency while also improving efficiency in this critical area.

Blockchain technology has revolutionized the way regulatory audits are conducted by providing an efficient means of creating transparent and verifiable records. With its ability to create detailed audit trails that can be easily traced back through every step in a process or transaction chain, blockchains have made it easier for auditors to verify compliance with regulations while minimizing errors during their assessments. This innovative approach is changing how we think about conducting business transactions altogether!

Enhanced Cybersecurity Measures

Advanced Cybersecurity Protocols:

Cybersecurity has become a critical concern for businesses as they strive to protect sensitive financial data from cyber threats. Blockchain technology offers an innovative solution by providing decentralized and cryptographic protection through its framework. By leveraging this unique feature of blockchain, revenue auditing can be enhanced with unparalleled security measures that reduce the risk of cyber-attacks significantly. With such robust defenses in place against potential breaches or hacks, companies can rest easy knowing their finances are safe from harm's way.

Incorporating Biometric Authentication into Access Controls:

Biometric authentication measures such as fingerprint or facial recognition are integrated within access controls to enhance cybersecurity. This ensures that only authorized personnel can gain entry into critical audit data and systems. By doing so, organizations protect themselves from unauthorized access attempts by hackers who may try stealing sensitive information. The use of biometrics adds an extra layer of security making it difficult for anyone else but the intended user to gain access. With this technology in place companies can rest assured knowing their most valuable assets remain secure at all times.

Continuous Cyber Threat Monitoring

Real time cyber threat detection is crucial for revenue auditors who rely on continuous monitoring systems to stay ahead of potential attacks. Automated tools analyze network activities and behaviors allowing them to quickly identify any suspicious activity or behavior that could indicate a security breach. With this technology in place, auditors can respond promptly before any damage occurs.

Auditors work closely with cybersecurity experts to ensure they are equipped against ever evolving threats. This collaboration involves regular assessments of security measures, implementation of robust protocols and proactive responses towards emerging risks. By doing so auditors stay ahead in the game when it comes to protecting sensitive information from potential breaches or attacks.

Integrating ESG Considerations into Your Business

ESG Reporting and Auditing: What You Need to Know

As part of their audit processes revenue auditors are increasingly incorporating environmental, social and governance (ESG) metrics. This means assessing the casinos impact on sustainability, corporate responsibility as well as good governance practices in comprehensive evaluations. By doing so they ensure that businesses operate responsibly while also promoting positive change towards a more sustainable future for all stakeholders involved.

ESG Compliance Audits: A new breed of audit is emerging that focuses on assessing casinos' adherence to ESG principles. These dedicated auditors provide stakeholders with valuable insights into the organization's commitment towards ethical and sustainable business practices. By undergoing such evaluations, companies can demonstrate their dedication towards upholding responsible corporate governance standards while also promoting transparency among investors who prioritize socially conscious investments.

Continued Professional Development

Regulatory Changes - Adapting

Continuous Professional Development: Revenue auditors prioritize ongoing professional development with a specific focus on staying up to date with regulatory changes. This ensures that they remain well informed about evolving gaming regulations and can adapt their auditing methodologies accordingly.

Within the fast-paced casino industry auditors must be able to adapt quickly in response to changing legislation. Professional development ensures that they can interpret and implement new regulations efficiently reducing the risk of noncompliance. This agility is crucial for maintaining a competitive edge within this dynamic field.

CASINO REVENUE AUDITING

Cross-Functional Training Initiatives:

Revenue auditors are encouraged to participate in cross functional training initiatives that enhance their versatility. This includes learning about non-gaming revenue auditing techniques as well as compliance procedures and collaborating with other departments within the casino operations. By developing this type of expertise across multiple areas they can effectively address any challenges presented by these complex environments.

Interdisciplinary collaboration is key for revenue auditors in today's casino industry. To achieve this goal training initiatives prioritize developing these skills among team members from various departments such as IT specialists and compliance officers. By fostering a collaborative approach to casino revenue auditing through interdepartmental cooperation the end result will be improved outcomes for all parties involved.

The future of casino revenue auditing is shaped by several factors including technological advancements, data analytics capabilities and regulatory technology solutions. Additionally enhanced cybersecurity measures are necessary to protect against potential threats while considering ESG factors adds another layer of complexity. Professional development remains crucial in navigating these emerging trends effectively ensuring transparency and integrity within the dynamic landscape of the gaming industry. With all this in mind those working as revenue auditors have a critical role ahead of them in maintaining trustworthiness among stakeholders.

Revenue Auditors will lose focus if they keep doing the same thing over and over. Their mind will fall into a predictable pattern and thus will start to miss clues and patterns they would normally find.

I once came across a pattern of a server who never turned in cash during their shift. Investigation revealed a theft problem, but the auditor never noticed this pattern till months later. So it is better to switch audits among the staff every so often to keep their edge. This also helps with cross training to cover staff shortages.

Fraud happens. There are many different types of schemes, so I will cover just a few.

Credit cards can be stolen by individuals, rings of individuals. They may try to buy gift cards via those cards and then cash those cards out immediately. Just remember that there is a 3 day period for credit cards to be funded to the casino, so liability is on the casino if this is allowed.

Slot machines can be vulnerable too. Look for high volumes of cash out without corresponding play.